Praise for *Every Connection Matters*

"This book is wise, heartfelt, and actionable. The Creekmores offer an invaluable resource for all educators based on their many years of experience."

—**Elena Aguilar**, author of *Onward: Cultivating Emotional Resilience in Educators* and CEO of Bright Morning

"In *Every Connection Matters*, Michael and Nita Creekmore have constructed the handbook on building relationships for every teacher and administrator. As educators, we must show students that we are more than just teachers, we are people who are interested in building strong relationships and deep connections with their families. Creating a joyful and engaging school begins with cultivating relationships built on trust. When that happens, school becomes a very special place for children. This book is a must-read for every teacher and leader."

—**Salome Thomas-EL**, EdD, award-winning principal, teacher, author, and speaker

"Relationships are at the heart of our happiness and our effectiveness, and in *Every Connection Matters*, the Creekmores show us how to take care of ourselves and collaborate with others. This book is a treasure trove of ideas, strategies, and activities for building, maintaining, and restoring relationships. Reading it caused me to feel both refreshed and inspired! I highly recommend this book to teachers and principals."

—**Thomas R. Hoerr**, PhD, author of *The Formative Five*

"Without healthy, strong, and varied relationships, a career in education would be long and lonely. In this book, authors Michael and Nita Creekmore offer strategies to ensure that doesn't happen. With a balanced mix of personal experiences, reflective questions, and research-based ideas, readers will learn how to develop and implement strong school-based relationships. Each unique chapter will compel teachers and leaders to bridge their own experiences with those of others, providing an opportunity to reflect how choices, demeanor, and mindset affect relationships in their schools and communities."

—**Jen Schwanke**, EdD, author, administrator, and educational consultant

"*Every Connection Matters* is not just a book; it's a guide for educators, administrators, and anyone invested in the well-being of our students. It reinforces the idea that fostering connections is a shared responsibility, and it offers practical strategies for cultivating these bonds. Michael and Nita Creekmore remind us that, ultimately, it's the connections we forge that make education not only possible but truly meaningful."

—**Amen Rahh**, award-winning educator and founder of K12 Crypto

"*Every Connection Matters: How to Build, Maintain, and Restore Relationships Inside the Classroom and Out* by Michael Creekmore and Nita Creekmore is an essential read for all educators. The authors compellingly outline the critical need for a variety of meaningful relationships in our schools. The book shines in its practicality, providing tangible exercises and useful tools for creating and preserving meaningful relationships. This is not just another book about the importance of connections; it's a roadmap for how to create them."

—**Lisa Westman**, ASCD Faculty Member and author of
Student-Driven Differentiation and *Teaching with Empathy*

"Michael and Nita represent what a true relationship should consist of: trust, support, and ultimately love. They exhibit these characteristics and much more and ultimately practice what they preach. This book is a testament of what they have and what we all should strive to achieve."

—**Leonard Galloway**, Director of Human Resources,
Anderson School District Five, Anderson, SC

Every
Connection
Matters

ASCD MEMBER BOOK

Many ASCD members received this book as a
member benefit upon its initial release.

Learn more at: **www.ascd.org/memberbooks**

Every Connection Matters

Matters

How to **Build, Maintain,**
and **Restore Relationships**
Inside the Classroom and Out

MICHAEL CREEKMORE
AND **NITA CREEKMORE**

ascd

Arlington, Virginia USA

2800 Shirlington Road, Suite 1001 • Arlington, VA 22206 USA
Phone: 800-933-2723 or 703-578-9600 • Fax: 703-575-5400
Website: www.ascd.org • Email: member@ascd.org
Author guidelines: www.ascd.org/write

Richard Culatta, *Chief Executive Officer;* Anthony Rebora, *Chief Content Officer;* Genny Oster-tag, *Managing Director, Book Acquisitions & Editing;* Stephanie Bize, *Acquisitions Editor;* Mary Beth Nielsen, *Director, Book Editing;* Liz Wegner, *Editor;* Thomas Lytle, *Creative Director;* Donald Ely, *Art Director;* Melissa Johnston/The Hatcher Group, *Graphic Designer;* Valerie Younkin, *Senior Production Designer;* Kelly Marshall, *Production Manager;* Shajuan Martin, *E-Publishing Specialist;* Kathryn Oliver, *Creative Project Manager*

PAPERBACK ISBN: 978-1-4166-3266-5   ASCD product #123010

PDF EBOOK ISBN: 978-1-4166-3267-2; see Books in Print for other formats.

Quantity discounts are available: email programteam@ascd.org or call 800-933-2723, ext. 5773, or 703-575-5773. For desk copies, go to www.ascd.org/deskcopy.

ASCD Member Book No. FY24-1 (Jan 2024 PSI+). ASCD Member Books mail to Premium (P), Select (S), and Institutional Plus (I+) members on this schedule: Jan, PSI+; Feb, P; Apr, PSI+; May, P; Jul, PSI+; Aug, P; Sep, PSI+; Nov, PSI+; Dec, P. For current details on membership, see www.ascd.org/membership.

Library of Congress Cataloging-in-Publication Data
Names: Creekmore, Michael, author. | Creekmore, Nita, author.
Title: Every connection matters : how to build, maintain, and restore relationships inside the classroom and out / Michael Creekmore and Nita Creekmore.
Description: Arlington, VA : ASCD, [2024] | Includes bibliographical references and index.
Identifiers: LCCN 2023040321 (print) | LCCN 2023040322 (ebook) | ISBN 9781416632665 (paperback) | ISBN 9781416632672 (pdf ebook)
Subjects: LCSH: Teaching—Social aspects—United States. | Teacher-student relationships—United States. | Parent-teacher relationships—United States. | Teacher-administrator relationships—United States.
Classification: LCC LC191.4 .C74 2024 (print) | LCC LC191.4 (ebook) | DDC 371.102/3—dc23/eng/20231017
LC record available at https://lccn.loc.gov/2023040321
LC ebook record available at https://lccn.loc.gov/2023040322

33 32 31 30 29 28 27 26 25 24   1 2 3 4 5 6 7 8 9 10 11 12

To Bryson, Aspen, Simone, and Eva: We hope you pick up this book one day and you are at least half as proud of us as we are of you. You remain the driving force behind Mommy and Daddy's work in improving school culture and relationships within education.

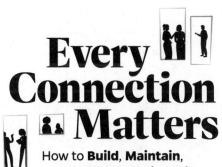

Every Connection Matters

How to **Build, Maintain,** and **Restore Relationships** Inside the Classroom and Out

Preface

A lot has been said about relationships in education—their power, the influence they may have among staff and students, and their effect on teacher retention. Relationships are multifaceted, however; good relationships are not the silver bullet that will fix everything in any or every school. At the same time, we can guarantee that relationships are an integral part of the solutions to many of the problems that schools face. Educators across the globe have discussed and expressed frustration with the suggestion that relationships are not the single cure for behavioral issues in the classroom or low morale within school buildings. However, we do suggest digging a little deeper into the quality of those relationships, including teachers' relationships with students and families, administrators' relationships with staff, and students' relationships with fellow classmates.

When we talk about relationships, we are speaking from years of personal and professional experience, research, and interviews with educators. We are not speaking about relationships to promote a buzz-word, fad, social media trend, or quick fix. As you read our book, we challenge you to reflect on the relationships in your school and how they affect your impact as an educator.

1 The School of Relationships

Dr. Yates is currently visiting schools in her district, where she has been the superintendent for the past four years. Every year, as she does her annual walk-throughs, she looks forward to visiting one particular school: BMR Middle School. As she and her administrative team enter the school, Dr. Yates reminds her team to observe the interactions and overall culture of the building. A small student leadership team is awaiting Dr. Yates and her colleagues in the main lobby. Without hesitation, all three students extend a warm welcome, and Mr. Smith, the school principal, makes small talk with the superintendent.

The walk-through, as always, is a notable success. Dr. Yates and her team meet with Mr. Smith to debrief and highlight observations. Dr. Yates opens by asking, "How do you do it? Every year I look forward to coming to BMR Middle because it seems like there is a certain magic going on here. What is it? And can you package it to give to a few other schools?" Mr. Smith smiles, says "Thank you," and offers a one-word answer: "Relationships!" He suggests that every relationship in the building may not have the same priority but holds equal weight. He explains, "We go about the business of relationship building the same way we go about teaching—wholeheartedly."

1

Why Relationships Are Important

Although a common belief asserts that each stakeholder in an education system and school is important, our daily tasks, duties, and responsibilities can sometimes lead us to forget about the importance of relationship building. Studies have long shown the impact of positive relationships on students' growth and overall development (Ed Trust & MDRC, 2021). However, recent studies suggest relationships also have an impact on the morale and effectiveness of educators (Greater Good in Education, n.d.). But here's the thing: relationships are not always easy. Some productive and positive relationships just come naturally, whereas others definitely require more work. Building, cultivating, and sustaining productive and positive relationships in a school building can be challenging. When you are working with a variety of educators, many factors help to develop a healthy school culture. Effective leadership, a supportive community, trust, and adaptability are contributors; however, none is more important than relationships (Greater Good in Education, n.d.).

Relationships are the foundation of the important work that we do. Without them, we cannot do our work as educators; it becomes null and void. But why do we think that is so? Human beings desire connection to each other because ultimately we are social beings. In his book *Social Intelligence: The New Science of Human Relationships*, Daniel Goleman (2007) writes, "Resonant relationships are like emotional vitamins, sustaining us through tough times and nourishing us daily" (p. 312).

That truth is no different within the walls of a school building; students and educators desire and need healthy relationships. Think of it like this: when you are building a house, or a school in our case, the first thing you want to do is set the foundation. That is what everything is built upon. Relationships are the foundation. The school has to withstand fierce storms and wild winds. When the foundation is firm and steady, amazing things can happen, making your job as an educator a little easier and allowing you to work in a more positive space, a happier place.

Relationships are the driving force in all we do. Most educators go into their respective fields not only because of the content they are teaching but also because of the relationships that are built in the process. Wang and Haertel (2000) state that many studies reveal that teachers are often isolated from their peers and other school professionals. To lessen teachers' feeling of isolation, the school day must include opportunities to interact. It is human nature to want to interact and build relationships with others. We all need that. Educators thrive when they work in an environment with positive, authentic relationships as the basis of the work they do each day. If they are thriving, those feelings feed into their teaching, affecting students in a positive way.

A study by Le Cornu (2013) showed that for some teachers early in their careers, relationships "fostered a sense of belonging and social connectedness. For others, it provided emotional and professional support. They reported coping better and feeling more confident when they experienced support from other teachers in the school including being frequently asked about their welfare and being offered help" (p. 4). Obviously teachers benefit from these types of connections. Connections are the key to building authentic relationships.

What Is a Connection?

Irina Damascan (2019) says a connection is "something you maintain and work on every day," whereas "being in a relationship is the result of that work and not a given." You can use connections with someone to help build, maintain, or restore relationships. They can be as simple as saying hello every morning to a colleague or giving a student a high five when you pass them in the hallway. Saying hello each day can set the stage for a conversation—another connection. Creating spaces to build connections with others is key. So how do you do that?

One way is to find a commonality with others—even something as minor as agreeing on looking forward to an upcoming break. You might mention the break in conversation, the other person comments, and the two of you share a laugh. But a connection can also be a celebration of your differences, such as rooting for opposite football teams, which may mean taking yourself out of your comfort zone.

Although these may seem like surface-level interactions, they help to build deeper connections that can develop as time goes on. They require taking the time to get to know others, to learn about the experiences of "the person behind the mask." We all know as we enter our school building that we show others the person we want them to see. Connections are about taking the time to create moments, to create meaning, and to get to know others in order to create relationships. Once that happens, a space opens for deeper-level connections, such as acknowledging a coworker who is experiencing burnout and attempting to help by discussing current workload and helping to identify ways to cope. On a more personal level, deeper-level connections might include being aware of the health of a colleague's family member or helping to plan a coworker's wedding or baby shower. Over time, cultivating and fostering surface-level connections can lead to these kinds of deeper-level connections.

From Connections to Relationships

Oxford Languages (n.d.) defines *relationship* as "the way in which two or more concepts, objects, or people are connected, or the state of being connected." The key concept here, as previously noted, is connection. No meaningful relationship occurs without a connection first being made. In Figure 1.1, each "bubble" represents an established, consistent connection, either surface- or deeper-level, that has been made. Those established connections can lead to meaningful relationships, which in turn, over time, become resilient relationships that can withstand inevitable storms.

FIGURE 1.1

Moving from Connections to Relationships

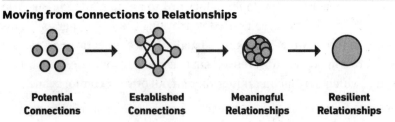

| Potential Connections | Established Connections | Meaningful Relationships | Resilient Relationships |

The challenge is that it is difficult to know if your relationship with someone is resilient until you have actually weathered a storm together. A good example of this is a major difference in opinion that leads both parties to walk away upset and in need of some space. The resilience sets in when the two parties come back together to talk and work through their differences. In doing this, both parties enter a realm of vulnerability—allowing themselves to know each other on an even deeper level, which increases the meaningfulness of the relationship with its resilience now discovered.

In school, our relationships with students, colleagues, and coworkers can help sustain our careers as educators. When that collaborative lesson you created with your colleagues rides the latest wave and everyone is coming to your team for assistance, your rockstar performance is shining through, and that relationship you've formed with your colleagues is magical.

"Magic" doesn't happen without relationships of one sort or another. Remember when you finally broke through to a student who had been struggling to understand a lesson, that feeling you experienced when the student finally understood? Magic! Years after you've taught little Johnny or little Kayla, you are walking through the grocery store, hear someone call your name, turn around, and see that same student, much older but with the same look of joy—that's magic! The magic is seeing the seeds that you sowed grow; it's the fruition of the meaningful work that you have poured into others and into yourself; it's a feeling of impact, of meaning, of accomplishment.

The magic created through productive relationships is what keeps educators in the field. When that feeling happens, it is important to snap a mental picture of it, to hold onto it, to write it down in a journal so that when you have hard days, you can remember that it isn't always hard.

During those difficult days that may include impromptu observations, defiant students, resistant parents, and low team morale, your relationships with your colleagues will help you pull through. Those remembered moments of magic will help you be resilient and build your strength as an educator. As you navigate your daily agenda, you have to remember that you can't operate in isolation. Figuratively speaking, if you're not connected to anyone, you could easily drift away and exist on your own island. Those relationships can keep you afloat and keep you from drowning.

Sometimes it may seem easier to stay on our islands because it's the land we can control; staying put seems easier and less stressful. But without relationships, no one wins. We cannot thrive as a community without making connections to establish relationships with others. We can't collectively become great if we stay in our individual silos. Connections transformed into relationships are what help us learn, grow, and be in community.

Whether you are new to the profession or simply new to the school, connections will make or break that honeymoon period you've been granted at the start. Most likely you became an educator because you care, you have a big heart, you love students, and you want to make an impact. But guess what? You will have no meaningful impact without making connections that lead to the building of relationships.

The Importance of Building, Maintaining, and Restoring Relationships

Building, maintaining, and restoring relationships—what we refer to as "BMR"—is what drives the work that educators do. It's that three-part combination that makes relationships strong.

Let's face it: we love to begin relationships on a high note, a positive note, one that gives everyone that happy, giddy feeling at the end of the day. However, as time goes on, disagreements with students, colleagues, leaders, or parents can be part of the relationship process and either strengthen or strain it. How can we achieve that strength? What can we plant into a relationship that needs to grow? How do we mend a relationship that needs to be repaired?

These are some of the questions that we will tackle in this book. We will provide answers to these tough questions, addressing relationships that seem hard to build and ones that seem unrepairable. An overarching theme of our approach is that it is never too late. There is always a space for a relationship to be cultivated. If we cannot see that space, we have to create it.

We all marvel at educators who can enter a room full of people they do not know yet and make connections—the ones who appear to have never met a stranger. They can walk into any situation and everyone loves them; it seems as though they have known everyone in the community forever. Sometimes you just want to pull them aside and ask, "How do you do that?" We observe these apparent "relationship gurus" in different settings to see if they have something or say something we don't. We wonder, how does this automatically happen?

You may often ask yourself, what if I'm *not* that type of educator? Can I still create relationships that grow and thrive? Of course you can! But it will take some work. Building positive, productive relationships with other educators, parents, and students will take effort on your part and the other party's as well. True, authentic relationships do not just happen; they are sown. The planting metaphor is apt: we know that when seeds are sown, it takes a while for them to germinate and grow. We just can't give up hope in the midst of that growth. We have to keep watering and tending to our relationship gardens.

What many educators do not realize is that from the moment you enter the school building, you are constructing or deconstructing relationships. Every time you come in contact with others, you are either building, maintaining, or restoring relationships. This is not to say that you cannot have a bad day or that there aren't some days when you just want to be alone and work through your own emotions and feelings. There is definitely a time for that. That is being human. However, when working with people, especially in the field of education, it is important to know that relationships matter each and every day.

Looking back at Figure 1.1, let's elaborate on the four stages in the shift from connections to relationships: potential connections, established connections, meaningful relationships, and resilient relationships.

Potential connections are random. You have potential connections with colleagues whom you bump into every so often and speak to based on the convenience of the moment. Potential connections include times when you speak briefly to a person in a hallway, share a joke with a teacher on your team, discover something in common that you have with a staff member in the front office, or casually chat with a colleague whom you just happened to sit beside when you arrived late to a meeting. Those are all ways that you can connect with others, ways that can lead to established connections. Potential connections fall into the "building" stage of a relationship.

Established connections are the daily and purposeful contacts you make with other individuals that allow you to know each other better. When you start a conversation with a colleague who just started serving on your same committee or speak to students who are not in your class, you are establishing connections. Like potential connections, established connections fall into the "building" stage of a relationship. They emerge from colleagues or students with whom you have regular conversations.

Meaningful relationships are the connections that stick. When you are aware of important details in colleagues' and students' lives, you probably have a meaningful relationship with them. They have chosen to share that information with you, and sometimes you share details of your lives with them. You talk to them regularly and have an emotional connection with them. Conversations are not always work related. During the good times and the hard times, you're there for each other. Meaningful connections fall into the "maintaining" stage of a relationship development.

Resilient relationships emerge after you and the other person have encountered an obstacle, expressed strong disagreement, or experienced a parting of ways, but the two of you are able to return to the relationship in a way that shows appreciation for each other. The most interesting part of resilient relationships is that you're never able to determine if your relationship is resilient until you have worked through any notable differences in opinion or belief, overcome drama, or resolved an argument. Resilient relationships fall into the "restoring" stage of a relationship that has been harmed.

Keys to a Successful Relationship

Relationships are complex, and, as we've noted, achieving successful relationships can seem like a daunting goal. It helps to have an understanding of four key components of successful relationships: trust, authenticity, respect, and communication.

Trust

Trust and relationships go hand and hand, and trust is something that is cultivated over time. There are occasions when we trust too soon and times when we don't trust soon enough. Past experiences play a significant role in the basic levels of trust. For example, if a new teacher comes into a school with different ideas and those ideas are shut down, the teacher may feel rejected and not as comfortable sharing ideas with teammates in the future. An initial feeling of trust has shifted into hesitancy.

As you begin a job at a new school, regardless of how many years you have been in the education profession, there are levels, or what we refer to figuratively as "rooms of trust," that you have to enter to cultivate resilient relationships. Figure 1.2 describes the characteristics of these spaces, or levels.

Authenticity

What does the term *authenticity* mean to you? It is the ability to be your 100-percent true self at all times and in every space. For some, that could be an accurate description. For others, this kind of authenticity is not what actually happens from day to day. Think for a moment about your behaviors, mannerisms, and conversations at home or with friends versus at work. Any difference? If there is no difference, we are celebrating you. That is exactly how it should be. However, for some, especially those in the global majority, that may not be the case. Terms such as *assimilating* and *code-switching* are sometimes used to describe survival behaviors that those of the global majority do to feel safe in work environments. Feeling psychologically safe enough to bring your full self into your workspace—to be fully who you are—facilitates the building of authentic relationships. Psychological safety is essential in bringing your full self into any environment and any relationship. But what can that look like? What does that feel like? We believe there are levels of authenticity in different contexts, and throughout this book, we will offer tips, reminders, and strategies on ways to bring your full, authentic self into the school of relationships.

FIGURE 1.2

The "Rooms" of Trust

Room	Level	Description
Front Lobby (Surface-Level Trust)	Professional	In a *literal* sense, the front lobby is where you greet someone at the door. You are showing your best self and are doing what is expected. In this *figurative* room, you are fulfilling your professional responsibility. Here you might have "surface-level trust"; you hold people accountable and assume that they will fulfill their professional responsibilities. For instance, if you as a teacher are required to complete lesson plans, the front lobby is where you believe other teachers will complete their lesson plans.
Break Room (Four-Walls Trust)	Team	The break room is where you and your colleagues have established rapport with each other; you are building community and supporting each other. You also are more open with your feelings about the ins and outs of the school. The break room often has a negative connotation; however, it is also where community building occurs. "Four-walls trust" refers to allowing yourself to be at your most vulnerable. At this level of trust, you share more than you would at the other levels. A high degree of psychological safety characterizes this space. For example, it is where you might learn that a colleague is having family problems, experiencing health issues, searching for a new job, or transferring to a different school. Four-walls trust often leads to friendship outside of the school.
School (In This Together Trust)	Community	Collectively, all the spaces within a school building can be considered one big room. Here is where the community comes together. Schoolwide trust is an "in this together" kind of trust. It can feel familial because most people are there for one another. Examples include helping someone new to your grade level or school, eating lunch with your team, or discussing grade-level or team plans. This is community-level trust that extends to everyone.

Respect

The definition of *respect* is due regard for the feelings, wishes, rights, or traditions of others. Opposing viewpoints prevail regarding the giving and receiving of respect. Some believe that you should receive respect before you give it, whereas others feel giving should come before receiving. Respect is something that can be subjective and culturally nuanced, and what it looks and sounds like within your school culture should be a topic for discussion.

Communication

Communication is a way to express your needs and wants and to convey information to one another. Many people have preferences on the type of communication used. Some prefer verbal, written, or nonverbal. But regardless, most agree that communication is important in relationship building. Without communication, relationships can break down. Some are never formed, and others are never repaired.

What Relationships Mean for Thriving Schools

Many schools that thrive are based on a strong foundation of positive, resilient relationships. Although all relationships within the school may not be in the resilient phase, intentionality and authenticity are embedded in the school culture, allowing teachers and staff to thrive. We acknowledge that not everyone in the school building may be holding hands and singing "Kumbaya," but strides are being made to build, maintain, and restore relationships in conjunction with educating students every day.

Are positive, productive relationships the answer to all the problems in a school? Absolutely not. But as you read, we believe you will see and come to agree that they are a strong component in the effort to create the changes we want to see in education.

Michael's Observations

During my years as a community mental health provider, I could always decode a school's culture when I entered the building. I did not use rocket science, nor did I use telepathic powers on the faculty and staff. The culture was evident by the way in which the students, teachers, and administrative staff interacted with each other. Sometimes it was revealed in vocal inflections, body language, and other nonverbal cues. Other times, it was the facial expressions and side conversations I might overhear. The connections between the people in the building were obvious. Some schools I entered were like Broadway musicals: everyone seemed to know their line and scene, and they interacted harmoniously with their cast members (coworkers and students). Other schools were like mosh pits at a heavy metal concert: lots of loud noise, nonstop frantic movement, and people who seemed preoccupied with their own need to be seen or heard.

The front office of any school always seemed to provide a snapshot of the school's inner workings. Bad connections and good connections shared a common thread; both were quite remarkable. Moreover, I can easily recall my favorite and least favorite colleagues based on the connection we did or did not share.

For better or for worse, the quality of the established connection is the determining factor in the quality of the relationship. We all have our favorite colleagues and coworkers, but we have to establish good working relationships with everyone—yes, *everyone*, even the most difficult coworker who has a master's degree in plucking your last nerve! Just remember when you encounter that coworker that it may take a little extra effort on your part to push the relationship forward. Doing so could look like initiating pleasantries or giving a compliment or just saying something nice to that person. However, prepare yourself to give and possibly not receive in return.

When I became a professional school counselor, it was like entering a world I'd only seen from the outside. Of course, I've seen the inner workings of many schools, but nothing compares to being in the trenches.

Everything was going smoothly during my first year—or so I thought! I was making connections and helping students and families. I was doing all the right things to be successful. Then came my first unpleasant encounter, and it was a doozy. I was walking down the hallway during dismissal when a colleague angrily approached me about a district-mandated guideline. I wasn't even responsible for it! Needless to say, a reasonable de-escalation did not occur. We had been mutually pleasant before this encounter. A connection had been established previously but not a meaningful relationship. With that said, do you think we were able to work through it, or move past it? In short, we moved past it but never worked through it. As a result, we reverted back to that "before" stage of an established connection. Our interactions became superficial and limited.

Nita's Observations

When entering the building to begin teaching at a new school, I always knew that my encounter with the office staff would help me gauge the overall school culture. I knew that if the office staff was pleasant, the culture of the school would likely be the same. Well, I always hoped so, anyway.

In this particular case, I walked in with a smile on my face and was ready to meet the front office staff to begin that positive relationship. But when I walked in, it seemed as though no one was there. Wait. No one at the front desks? As I stood there waiting, I got a brief hello from a lady who seemed to be running around looking for something. Now, I am a new teacher in this building. I could have looked at this situation and totally taken it negatively. I could have said to myself, Is this how this year is going to go? But I did not. The staff was obviously busy. I didn't know what had occurred before I walked through those doors. I sat down and waited for a few seconds, and then I got up and said, "Hello. My name is Nita Creekmore. I am the new teacher on the

1st grade team. Do you need me to help with anything?" At once, the lady, who happened to be the receptionist, stopped in her tracks and welcomed me with open arms and congratulated me on my new position.

Here's the thing. At that moment, I made a connection with the receptionist. At that moment, I chose to step out of my comfort zone of assumptions, and I made a connection. Part of making connections with people is stepping out of our comfort zones, releasing assumptions and how we think relationships *should* work, and instead doing what we feel is right.

Relationships aren't scripted or forced upon us by others; they just happen. However, they happen when we put our pride aside and decide to create a connection—to be intentional about building relationships through those connections. Building relationships is about intentionality. When I decided to introduce myself and ask if help was needed, I showed the receptionist at my new school that I *saw* her. I showed her that I was willing to pull up my sleeves and help, and I showed her my compassion. A connection was made because I decided to step out and put down the first brick in the building—the building of relationships.

Reflective Questions

- What are some ways you create connections in your school community?
- How do you build relationships within your school?
- Who do you think bears the responsibility for relationship building at your school?
- What are some examples of relationships that you have fostered in your school community? What are some potential relationships that you have not fostered?

2 Teacher-to-Self Relationships

Mr. Burnett is a 10th grade science teacher who has been working at Bethel High School for 11 years. He has put his all into Bethel and his students. In addition to teaching science, Mr. Burnett is dedicated to tutoring students after school. He is well respected, admired by many, and seems to have a good relationship with colleagues and students alike.

Mr. Burnett's positive reputation led to him being asked to help out with the school basketball program—specifically, to assist coaches during the season by keeping stats. When the winter holidays approached, Mr. Burnett was staying at school longer. Holiday tournament season was in full swing, which meant practices were longer and more intense. At home, he spent much of his time entering grades for his classroom students so that his records would stay up to date. With less down time and more work, he started feeling less energetic and more lethargic. When he went to a doctor's appointment, he was diagnosed with a severe respiratory illness.

Due to a substitute teacher shortage in the Bethel school district, Mr. Burnett could not find someone to cover his class. Even though his doctor warned him of the risk of returning to work, Mr. Burnett's guilt over not "being there" for the students and his inability to find a substitute led him to return to work prematurely.

On his second day back at school, Mr. Burnett sat down to take a break during third period and passed out. He was hospitalized for the next two weeks, using up all his sick days. What could he do now? Although he appreciated the steady stream of get-well cards that flooded his hospital room, he couldn't help but wonder what he could've done differently to avoid his situation.

Why the Teacher-to-Self Relationship Is Important

We realize the concept of a "teacher-to-self relationship" may seem strange at first. After all, we typically think of relationships as referring to our connections to other people. However, before we connect and develop relationships with others, we all have a relationship with ourselves in terms of how we judge ourselves and our behavior, how we think about the events and people that affect our outlook on life, and how we address our emotional, mental, and physical well-being. Considering these various factors, the teacher-to-self relationship is all about self-care.

Educators are often thought of as the professionals with the biggest hearts, always willing to go the extra mile and to sacrifice whatever it takes for their students and school community—even if "whatever it takes" means themselves. Self-care has generally been a back-burner topic or thought of as fluff in the education profession. However, an article in the *Washington Post* stated that teachers, in general, "were more likely to report experiencing frequent job-related stress and symptoms of depression than the general population" (Streeter, 2021).

Even before the pandemic, educators experienced an overwhelming amount of stress, enduring the effects of a long-held norm characterized by relatively low pay, long work hours, and expectations of dedication (Streeter, 2021). During the pandemic, the expectations stretched further. Educators were thought of as babysitters for children while still trying to care for themselves and their own families. Whether in times of crisis or "normal" circumstances, many educators have experienced what is commonly known as *burnout*.

American psychologist Herbert Freudenberger coined the term "burnout," using it in a paper titled "Staff Burn-Out" (1974), which described the negative effects of severe stress among people in the "helping professions," such as doctors and nurses. Later, Freudenberger and coauthor Gail North (1985) developed a 12-stage model to identify the many facets of burnout and how we, in no particular order, cycle through them.

Many argue that a large number of educators are burned out; however, the term more frequently used now is the "Sunday Scaries." The Sunday Scaries is generally described as an intense fear or anxiety that educators—and others—experience on the Sunday before returning to work. The truth of the matter is burnout is the umbrella and Sunday Scaries is the most highlighted symptom. The angst teachers feel during the Sunday Scaries doesn't fully encompass many educators' current state of mind. The irony is that when the pandemic shut down schools, most educators felt the appreciation and gratitude exhibited by the masses. They hoped those sentiments would propel the education profession in a new direction that would include higher salaries, fewer non-teaching demands, lower student-to-teacher ratios, and maybe even an increase in the number of school-based mental health professionals. Unfortunately, none of these things have changed on a grand scale.

As a result, many educators are more stressed, overwhelmed, and beyond burned out. Situations such as Mr. Burnett's, described in the vignette that opened this chapter, have become more commonplace. The unforeseen demands required to overcome countless obstacles, inequities, and systemic biases have served as proverbial quicksand for educators who once loved their jobs.

A great way to process feelings and emotions about job satisfaction is by reflection and by asking the essential questions. Let's dig more deeply into what burnout looks like and feels like with what we call the Burnout Checklists. The question, specifically, is "What can educators and leaders do to acknowledge and work through burnout?"

We have created two checklists—one for teachers and other school staff and one for school leaders. School staff members in any position can use the Burnout Checklist for Self-Reflection (Figure 2.1) to help determine their level of burnout and potentially work out a plan to address it. Ideally, this form should be administered electronically via methods such as Google Docs, which makes it easier to gather school-wide statistics. School leaders can administer the Burnout Checklist for Schools (Figure 2.2) to determine the level of whole-staff burnout. These forms are intended to jumpstart action and initiate productive conversation in order for individual and systemic change to occur. We recommend using them in October or November, which is usually when educators start to feel drained. You may also choose to use these forms in early March, another stressful time for educators due to preparation for standardized testing as well as spring fever, the time of year that the warm weather starts to return and students may be disengaged or exhibit heightened behaviors amid the mad dash to the end of the year.

Ways to Build, Maintain, and Restore the Teacher-to-Self Relationship

We define *self-care*—the essence of the teacher-to-self relationship—as any activity that a person deliberately completes to ensure mental, emotional, and physical well-being. Every educator has a breaking point. When it's time to go to a physician for something other than routine care, our bodies give off signals such as headaches, fatigue, mood changes, sleeplessness, greater anxiety, decreased or increased appetite, increased irritability, and so on. When this happens, we need some type of treatment to address the symptoms. Self-care can often be the prescription, something that we have to do for ourselves to combat work stress. It may not be the complete remedy, but it can most certainly help manage those difficult times when work and our personal life become hard and overwhelming (Baker, 2020).

Build

Building a self-care plan is an individual matter, and so it's important to determine what *you* need to take care of *yourself.* But how do you do that? How do you know what your body needs to get started on self-care?

FIGURE 2.1

Burnout Checklist for Self-Reflection

Question	Answer
Do you feel anxious or overwhelmed on most Sundays before returning to work?	
Have you been feeling more tired than usual? If so, can you identify the cause?	
Have you been on edge on a daily basis? If so, at what time of day?	
Do you feel constantly overwhelmed? If so, what do you think contributes to that feeling?	
Have you needed to take time off work more than usual?	
Has your passion for teaching decreased or your view of teaching become negative?	
Are previously lighthearted jokes and comments about education no longer funny?	
Have you grown resentful toward your school?	
Do you isolate yourself at school?	
Have you recently considered a career change due to dissatisfaction in your current position?	
Has your physical or mental health been affected?	

FIGURE 2.2

Burnout Checklist for Schools

Question	Answer
Do you feel supported at school? Yes or no? Please explain.	
Do you feel valued and appreciated? Yes or no? Please explain.	
Do you feel our school morale is high or low? Please explain.	
Do you enjoy coming to work most days? Yes or no? Please explain.	
Do you feel that your time is valued, including time for things such as professional learning, team meetings, RTI meetings, and so on? Yes or no? Please explain.	
What professional learning do you think would be valuable to you right now?	
Is there something in your work schedule you feel leadership can take off your plate? If so, please explain.	
What are some areas of growth for our administrative team?	
What are some areas of strength in our administrative team?	

The first step is the decision to put yourself first and to understand that self-care is not selfish. It is essential in order to flourish and be your best self. This process is one of self-exploration. To know what works for you, you have to get to know yourself in terms of three major components of self-care: emotional wellness, mental wellness, and physical wellness.

Build: Emotional Wellness

A key to emotional wellness is what we call "protecting your peace." It is hard to manage our emotions when we purposely take in negative things that drain our emotional energy. For instance, reducing the amount of time spent on social media can improve our emotional state. Simply avoiding videos that are likely to have a negative effect helps prevent us from becoming upset or vicariously traumatized. Sometimes we simply have to stop scrolling.

Our mood is often influenced by what we see, what we hear, and the interactions we have with others. During those times when we're feeling a little down, something as simple as listening to some upbeat music may help put a little pep in our step.

We can also try to surround ourselves with people who have a positive rather than negative effect on our emotional wellness. For example, we all have friends who may require more of our time, attention, and energy than others; but if those friends constantly leave us feeling exhausted, it may be time to reevaluate that friendship. It is OK to prioritize yourself and say no when necessary, even to a friend. Make sure to avoid toxic people and toxic situations. Sometimes our "friends" bring toxic vibes, often unknowingly. When you feel your mood changing from positive to negative, there's usually a situation, an incident, or a person that serves as a catalyst for that abrupt change.

Of course, there are many other ways to build emotional wellness. The following are a few examples.

Find a laugh, every day. Whether it is going out with friends, making a phone call, watching a movie, streaming a new show, reading a book, or having a virtual chat with family and friends you enjoy engaging with, find time to laugh. Laughter is good for the soul!

Reduce social media consumption. Social media affects us all, in many different ways. Some of us find ourselves in comparison traps; others watch videos that cause secondary trauma due to the "trauma dumping" of others—the sharing of trauma at an inappropriate time with someone who may not be equipped to process it.

Learn something new. Educators are "forever learners." We love learning. Take time to learn something different. Have you always wanted to learn how to play an instrument? What about learning how to knit? Learning how to do new things can be the necessary redirection that changes your overall mood.

Embrace all that is good. Start a gratitude journal. Each morning, write about what you are grateful for and what is going right. Studies show that the human mind often defaults to negative thoughts. Combine that tendency with people's natural inclination to try to fix the wrong and you're left with little time to embrace what is going well. Embrace the good!

Set healthy boundaries. Make sure you are establishing healthy boundaries for yourself. Do not put too much on your plate. Be brave enough to decline opportunities that may send you over the edge.

Build: Mental Wellness

The pandemic and its aftermath have led to the most challenging time in the lives of many educators, taking a significant toll on the mental health of many. Citing several research studies, Valosek and colleagues (2021) report that "stressors that may be contributing to teacher burnout include classroom management problems due to student misbehavior, high workloads, feeling of time pressure, excessive administrative tasks, and other organization factors."

It's often recommended that we go to a doctor when we feel physically ill, right? Why shouldn't the same be said when we're not feeling well mentally? There is no shame in seeking help from a mental health professional. Doing so is actually a sign of strength and a wonderful display of self-awareness. Unfortunately, there's still a lot of scrutiny and stigma around mental health, and some people consider it a "bad word." Hopefully this situation will change in the years ahead, but in the meantime, please know that these misperceptions shouldn't prevent addressing the mental health needs of countless educators.

If you decide to seek professional help, use your health insurance and school district Employee Assistance Program (EAP) to help you locate a suitable therapist. Call your insurance provider to find in-network professionals who specialize in areas of expertise related to your particular concerns. For example, if you feel noticeably more anxious whenever you are at work, you may want to seek the help of a licensed professional who specializes in anxiety-related issues.

School districts across the United States provide EAP services free of charge to address psychosocial and emotional needs through counseling. For many people, therapy sessions are one of the few times when they are able to tell their story without judgment. Sometimes just being able to tell your story, grapple with hard truths, and gain insight from a knowledgeable professional is all that you need in order to move in a new and positive direction. Remember, you get out of therapy whatever you put into it. If you are vague or omit vital information for fear of judgment, progress may be minimal.

Aside from consulting a mental health professional, you can take "smaller" steps. You may find the following suggestions helpful.

Feel your feelings. Your feelings are valid. It's OK to acknowledge them. Get a journal and write down how you feel. If writing is not your thing, start a personal vlog. When something is bothering you, speak up. Don't allow the weight of the moment to bring you down by holding in your feelings.

Take time to journal. Taking time to journal allows you to reflect on day-to-day experiences. It can help you to sort through emotions—including those feelings mentioned in the previous point—and to flesh out anything that may be causing stress. Journaling often makes things clearer, as you record information that can help you to understand what's going on in your life. Taking time to journal every day or once a week is a practice worth adding to your routine.

Find time to meditate. Meditation is the act of using mindfulness to focus on the present moment. It allows us to gain control over our wandering thoughts and begin to have clarity, and it increases calmness. There are many ways to meditate. Some practice meditation silently, whereas others may incorporate the sounds of nature or chanting affirmations. Even five minutes of meditation can help with mental health and increase self-care.

Join an educator support group. A support group may be a virtual gathering or an in-person gathering in your school community. Joining such a group provides a way to vent frustrations, get fresh ideas, and feel seen. Being in community with others can reassure you that you are not alone on your island. Just being able to connect with others can help to increase your well-being.

Build: Physical Wellness

Often when people struggle with their emotional and mental self-care, the effects manifest in their physical health as well. In fact, physical health and mental health are closely related. Good mental health can lead to improvements in your physical health, and the reverse is true as well (Good Therapy, 2022). When one is off kilter, the other is greatly affected. That is why it is so important to continue to be self-aware when you are feeling physically off. We educators tend to check in with everybody else and neglect ourselves. We may be attentive when the check engine light comes on in our vehicles but neglect to do anything when our body's "check engine light" comes on.

It is important to prioritize our physical bodies as part of our wellness plan. For example, sometimes we simply need to get out of the school building when we've been there all day. It can become physically draining to be a part of endless committee meetings that require additional work hours in the building we've been in for eight hours or more. Taking care of ourselves may mean sometimes saying no. "No" can be a complete sentence that preserves our physical health and activates our self-care as well.

What are some other ways to help jumpstart improvement in your physical health? Consider the following suggestions.

Establish work cutoff times. Today's educators face increased accountability, responsibility, duties, tasks, and overall workload, but the time in which they are expected to deal with all these things has not changed. Regardless of the lack of additional time, you have to establish times you begin and end each day. In other words, identify a "hard stop" for ending your work. Some of our tasks as educators are similar to laundry: it's always there, it's ongoing, and you never feel like you're through with it. Be OK with *not* finishing everything before you leave your school building. When you notice you're the first person to arrive and the last person to leave—every day—you are in trouble.

Exercise regularly. Even though working out may not be one of your desired self-care action steps, consider this: exercising regularly has been scientifically proven to combat and decrease the likelihood of anxiety and depression. When we exercise, our bodies release endorphins that make us feel energetic and serve as a natural mood boost (Mayo Clinic Staff, 2022). Examples of endorphin-producing activities are walking, dancing, hiking, jogging, running, jumping rope, jumping jacks, mountain climbing, jump-squats, kickboxing, burpees, HIIT (high-intensity interval training) workouts, step aerobics, yoga, and Pilates, among others.

Improve your sleep hygiene. Getting a good night's sleep is important for both physical and mental health, improving productivity and overall quality of life (Suni & Vyas, 2023). Some ways to improve your sleep are to cut off cell phone time one hour before bedtime, set a schedule for sleeping, create a bedtime routine, use a noise machine, and dedicate your bedroom as a place for relaxation and rest.

Establish healthy eating habits. Eating healthy is an obvious way to help improve your physical health. Making wiser choices in food consumption can help with this. Prepping meals ahead of time can decrease the likelihood of unhealthy meal choices that can happen during the day. Eliminating late-night eating will help as well. This is not to say you should never have a treat. But getting into a healthy eating routine is an important step in improving your physical health. If you think this step might be a challenge for you, consider consulting a dietician.

You can incorporate the suggestions provided here for emotional, mental, and physical well-being into an individualized self-care plan that becomes the core element in the "build" phase of the teacher-to-self relationship. You should start creating your self-care treatment plan as soon as possible—even before you think you may need one—so that it becomes a part of your daily routine and not crisis care, which is a brief recovery period to help you return to your baseline level of functioning (Creekmore & Creekmore, 2020). Develop a schedule that works for you. Be intentional. Intentionality is key!

We have created a template to use in developing your self-care plan (see Figure 2.3). Filling it out requires that you first dig into what your symptom is (e.g., Sunday Scaries). Next, consider what feeling or emotion it brings up for you (e.g., nervousness, anxiety). Then, determine an action step to take to address it and how frequently you will do it (e.g., do yoga or another type of exercise for one hour, three times a week). Afterward, take time to reflect on how you felt afterward (e.g., "After doing yoga, I felt tired but calm and rejuvenated," or "I didn't like this yoga session; it was too strenuous. I might try another instructor next time"). Based on your reflection, you may want to readjust your plan. It's important to remember that the development process will involve trial and error. You may try some things that you realize don't match what you like or who you are. On the other hand, your attempt to broaden your horizons may bring joy that you never expected. Specific components may change over time due to changing life circumstances and individual growth.

Being able to keep up with your self-care on your own might be a daunting task. What seemed easy at first may become challenging, making it tempting to push self-care further and further down on the to-do list. This reality is why it's important to identify accountability partners—people you trust, who have your best interests at heart and know you fairly well. Take time to think about who your accountability partner(s) could be and add their names to the template.

When you think of self-care, you may wonder what makes one treatment plan better, more effective than another. In our view, incorporating all three areas—emotional, mental, and physical wellness—is the key to creating an effective treatment plan. Consider that there will be times when you feel physically exhausted; you'll need to sit down and rest. At other times, you may need to increase your physical activity to help boost the release of the "feel good" chemicals in your brain—the endorphins. Sometimes work and social situations, friendships and other relationships, or the state of society will upset

FIGURE 2.3

My Self-Care Treatment Plan

Accountability Partner(s):			
Symptom	**Feeling/Emotion**	**Action Step**	**Frequency**
Reflection:			
Symptom	**Feeling/Emotion**	**Action Step**	**Frequency**
Reflection:			
Symptom	**Feeling/Emotion**	**Action Step**	**Frequency**
Reflection:			
Symptom	**Feeling/Emotion**	**Action Step**	**Frequency**
Reflection:			
Symptom	**Feeling/Emotion**	**Action Step**	**Frequency**
Reflection:			

you, causing you emotional distress. Your level of anxiety, sadness, doubt, or fear may significantly impede your daily functioning, which may result in the need to speak to a licensed professional. Using your self-care treatment plan will help you identify your areas of need and address them with appropriate actions. By targeting those three specific areas, your self-care treatment plan adopts a holistic approach to mending your mind, body, and soul.

Above all, don't forget the most important fact about self-care: it's an *action*. It only works if you *do* it, which brings us to the next phase in the process: maintaining self-care.

Maintain

Maintenance is essential to the overall success of self-care. You may get sidetracked, be forced to minimize the time spent on self-care, or forego your plan altogether. It happens and is not unusual. However, your accountability partner can help you get right back in the groove.

Obviously if the plan is effective, there's no need to change or adjust an action step. Stick with what's working. However, if your plan is not working, it's time to readjust.

In maintaining your self-care, remember that the plan is *yours*. At times you may try something new that works for someone else but doesn't work for you. That's OK. Try not to compare yourself to others. The comparison trap can lead to the complete opposite of what you are trying to accomplish in taking care of yourself. It can leave you feeling as though you are doing too little or too much of this or that. Let that feeling go and focus on taking care of *you*. The following suggestions can help you maintain your self-care plan:

Check in with your accountability partner(s). Take time to check in with the folks who care about you and your overall well-being. These are the people who will support you and help you to stay on track.

Revise and adjust your self-care treatment plan as needed. Look over your plan periodically. If it's working, continue on the same path. If it's not working, take the time to revise it. Remember that your plan is not set in stone; you can change it any time it's not meeting your needs. It's like a lesson plan for yourself—one of the most important lesson plans you'll write.

Enforce your boundaries. Some people won't like it when you begin to prioritize yourself. Perhaps they benefited from you working yourself to the point of depletion. But setting clear boundaries for yourself will aid in your overall health.

Share your self-care accomplishments with a friend. Share your wins! Doing so will help you to celebrate yourself. Taking the time to share is important. You deserve to celebrate the work you have done to ensure that you are in a healthy space.

Restore

One of the first steps in restoring self-care is to take inventory of how everything is working. Scheduled breaks within your school district calendar are an ideal time for an overall reflection. Look back on your successes as well as your failures. Determine what you can improve and identify how to make your self-care treatment plan better.

Restoring your self-care may look a little different at various times, depending on the severity of your burnout. Sometimes a short getaway will cure your ailments. Other times require something more—perhaps deciding to leave your current position or, in extreme cases, leave the field of education altogether. These latter options have been a topic of wide discussion over recent years. As previously mentioned, the process of restoring often involves reflecting. For educators, the ultimate reflection question may be "Is it time to leave my school?" or "Is it time to leave the profession?" Here's a tip: when you get to a point where your lows consistently outweigh your highs and you feel physically, emotionally, and mentally drained every time you leave your school building, it may be time to cue your outro music. You may need to seek employment at another school or district or, if you're not ready to take that step, consider pursuing a different role in your school building. Sometimes a change in grade level or position can help eliminate the feelings of burnout, stagnation, or not feeling valued. In more extreme situations, situations that take a consistently considerable toll on your emotional and mental well-being, seeking a career outside of the traditional K–12 school system may be necessary. The restoration of the teacher-to-self relationship requires doing your own work to figure out what the next step in your professional journey will be.

* * *

Figure 2.4 highlights the main points related to building, maintaining, and restoring the teacher-to-self relationship. You can use it as a guide and reminder of ways to make self-care a priority.

FIGURE 2.4

Ways to Build, Maintain, and Restore the Teacher-to-Self Relationship

Build	Maintain	Restore
• Complete the Burnout Checklist for Self-Reflection (Figure 2.1). • Complete your self-care treatment plan (Figure 2.3). • Find out what works for you in establishing self-care. • Establish boundaries around your work time.	• Check in with your accountability partner and review your self-care treatment plan. • Revise and adjust your self-care treatment plan as needed. • Enforce your work-time boundaries. • Try to avoid the comparison trap. • Share your self-care wins with a friend.	• Continue the check-in process. • Reevaluate and reflect on your self-care. • Revise and adjust your self-care treatment plan if it is not working. • Continue to share your self-care wins with a friend. • Reevaluate your employment opportunities.

Observations from Michael and Nita

Michael's Observations

I remember being in graduate school, working on my master's degree, and hearing my professor say, "I want you all to remember, helping professions like therapy, social work, and education can be some of the most thankless professions. You will need to learn how to take care of yourself and learn what you can do to overcome those tired and burnt-out moments, 'cause they're gonna happen."

At that moment I understood that statement as much as I could but not fully. Even though I was working a full-time job at a psychiatric residential treatment facility, completing internship hours at the same facility (in a different program), and completing other courses, I was fresh—I was new, unseasoned, a rookie to burnout. I say all of this now because as I reflect on my own self-care journey, I realize I naively thought the amount of work or the sheer number of tasks, duties, and responsibilities had a direct correlation to burnout. I was so wrong!

It took me a little over a decade to experience that "I can't do this anymore" feeling. I was working for a behavioral healthcare organization and had just completed a phone call about insurance benefits when I found myself questioning my overall effectiveness. I thought, "How can I have a greater impact?" Sure, I would always give insurance subscribers insight and tips to help them maximize their insurance benefits, but that nagging feeling of unfulfillment grew larger and larger. After years of working from home, I was burnt out. I had worked in other behavioral health departments within the company and was viewed as an asset, but I couldn't shake that nagging feeling. No matter what I did outside of work, my job was consistently dragging me emotionally and mentally, which led to physical implications. My duties as a behavioral health clinical care advocate were far fewer than all of the duties and responsibilities I had experienced as a graduate student, full-time employee, and intern; yet somehow I was officially burned out. I felt it coming, tried to use different action steps with hopes that my self-care would alleviate the negative feelings I had developed toward my job.

Nothing worked. I realized I needed to leave the position, and I took the necessary steps to prepare myself for a transition, a change in employment. One thing I can say: I never stopped learning, never stopped obtaining certifications and taking advantage of self-driven professional learning. I had prepared myself for the transition into school counseling. For me, preparation was always an integral part of combating burnout.

Nita's Observations

Self-care was something that was almost nonexistent for me for about 7 of the 13 years I was a classroom teacher. I worked myself to the bone most days. Then as a mother, I came home and did the same. Many times I would fall asleep watching a family movie or just was not as present as I should have been with the people I love. The situation wasn't healthy. I wasn't finding time in my day for myself. Everything was about my family or my students.

Although it seems like a great and admirable thing to put family and students first, that's not the case if you're working yourself to exhaustion. I was drained. I was tired of feeling like I had nothing left to give. I took control and a necessary first step and began working out. I made sure I joined a gym that provided childcare, because I didn't want my children to be an excuse for not exercising. I began to take time out to occasionally go to dinner with friends. I also got back into writing and journaling. I began to pour more into myself and what I needed. I began to feel better—happier. I remember even taking Zumba classes and truly getting into dancing, which brought me joy outside of my family and school.

Here is what I learned: without taking care of yourself first, you cannot be the best version of you. It's impossible. When you are burning the candle on both ends, you become depleted. Once I began to reclaim myself physically, mentally, and emotionally, I actually became better. I was a better wife, mother, teacher, and colleague, experiencing less anxiety and stress.

This is not to say that stressful situations didn't and don't arise, because they do. But I was and am now able to be better equipped to cope when those situations do arise. I am able to check in on myself. I often do a mental check-in at certain times throughout the year when I know that stress increases for me. I check in at the beginning of the school year, because we all know that getting ready to start a new school year involves a high level of stress, and in November/December, when the holidays are coming up and I am ready for a break. These check-ins lower my anxiety, and I am able to be my best self. I make sure I am following my own plan and completing tasks that I know lower my level of stress. I check in again at about March and at the end of the year as well. These mental check-ins help me to stay the course. They help me to be my best self—for myself; and that, in turn, helps me to show up fully for others.

Reflective Questions

- What are some things you do for self-care that have been beneficial to your emotional, mental, and physical well-being?
- What are some things from this chapter that you would like to implement, and why?
- What is one step you can take to prioritize your self-care?
- Burnout can look different for educators at various stages in their career. How do you know when you are burned out? What can you do to combat or minimize it?

3 Teacher-to-Student Relationships

At the beginning of each year, Mrs. Sellers has a "Getting to Know You" activity, during which students bring in items that represent who they are today, such as pictures of their family and things that represent their hobbies. Lydia, one of the students, began her turn by sharing a family photo that showed her with her two moms and her baby brother. Mrs. Sellers asked who the second woman was, assuming it was Lydia's older sister. Lydia explained that it was her other mom. Mrs. Sellers gasped and quickly moved on to the next student, cutting short Lydia's sharing time. The next student asked Lydia why she had two moms and where her dad was. Mrs. Sellers started feeling uncomfortable, her face turning beet red as she told the kids that the conversation was not appropriate. Another student raised his hand and asked why the conversation was inappropriate. Mrs. Sellers responded by saying it "just is!" She could feel herself getting angry. When she looked over and saw Lydia tearing up, she decided to send her to the school counselor.

Why Teacher-to-Student Relationships Are Important

The teacher-to-student relationship is one that truly focuses on why most of us got into education. We may have taken different paths to the profession, but we landed at the same spot for the same reasons. We pursued teaching as a career because we love kids; we love to teach; we love to see kids grow emotionally, intellectually, and socially; and we want to make a difference. Those reasons represent our initial motivation and state of mind. But the question is, what sustains us? After we have worked for 1, 2, 10, 20 years, what is the main factor holding us in place? It is the relationship factor; the relationships that we form with students are what keeps us coming back year after year. It is that connection that helps us know that we are indeed making a difference.

Teacher-to-student relationships are important because without a solid, positive relationship, learning cannot happen. In her 2013 TED Talk titled "Every Kid Needs a Champion," educator Rita Pierson stated, "Kids don't learn from people they don't like." The accuracy in that statement is profound. The students we teach—no matter their background, identity, or family circumstances—want a connection. They want a relationship with their teacher that is positive, and teachers should want the same thing in return.

In the vignette that opened this chapter, Mrs. Sellers had an activity that was intended to help her get to know her students and begin building relationships. However, it did not go as planned when she began hearing about their actual lives and families—particularly Lydia's family. Discovering that Lydia had two moms left Mrs. Sellers visibly unnerved; she had a difficult time listening to Lydia's explanation about her family members. There could be many reasons for Mrs. Sellers's reaction, but regardless, the impact was greater than the intent. She may have wanted to have some space to think through the discussion, but Lydia felt the immediate effect. She was clearly upset, and Mrs. Sellers missed an opportunity to check in with her student. This situation could have multiple effects on the relationship between Mrs. Sellers and Lydia as the year goes on.

An *Education Week* article titled "Why Teacher-Student Relationships Matter" reports on an analysis of 46 studies, which found that "strong teacher-student relationships were associated in both the short- and long-term with improvements on practically every measure schools care about: higher student academic engagement, attendance, grades, fewer disruptive behaviors and suspensions, and lower school dropout rates" (Sparks, 2019, para. 7). A strong teacher-student relationship is the factor that can change the trajectory of a student's educational path (Ansari et al., 2020; Gehlbach et al., 2012; Rimm-Kaufman & Sandilos, 2015).

Building a strong relationship with students from the beginning adds a level of psychological safety to the classroom. The feeling of being taken care of and knowing that a teacher is there for them allows students to be themselves in a psychologically safe environment, to learn freely and thrive in their learning. Students who feel their teacher likes them and holds their well-being as a priority will push themselves as they never have before. These are the students who keep trying, enjoy coming to school, want to do well, and continue to foster the relationship with their teacher even after the school year has ended. On the other hand, when students feel a teacher does not like them or no positive relationship is established, they will not strive to be their best selves in that classroom. They may withdraw, do the bare minimum, or count the days until the end of the school year.

When we think about the teachers who had the most influence on our lives, we probably think less about the content they taught us and more about how they valued who we are, poured effort into us, and truly cared. Those are the teachers we want to visit when we get older, the ones who changed the game for us.

What are some things that those impactful teachers do for students that make such a difference? The answer involves two critical factors: trust and authenticity.

Trust

Trust is at the heart of any thriving relationship and plays a major role when you are dealing with students. Students build positive relationships with those they trust; it is a huge factor for them. It means doing what you say you are going to do, following through with commitments, being there for them, and accepting them for who they are. If trust is shaken, it is hard to restore. It's not impossible, but it may take a while. When students trust you, they will open up, they will talk to you about their feelings and emotions, and they will want to be a part of the classroom community.

One way for teachers to establish trust with students is to show their own vulnerability. In her article "Building Trust with Students—Even Before Class Starts," Alicia Burns (2022) states that "when we show our students that we sometimes struggle or that we don't always have all the answers, it reinforces that we are all human." What better way to build trust than to show our students that teachers are also human and make mistakes?

Once you have students' trust and they know that you care about them, you have something to cherish and not take for granted. Trust is fragile; it is hard to build and crumbles easily.

Authenticity

An important factor that contributes to trust is authenticity. Being yourself and allowing your students to also bring their full selves into the learning community is important to building a strong teacher-to-student relationship. If students feel that they cannot be their authentic selves with you, the relationship will not grow. The reverse is true as well. Sometimes teachers try to turn themselves into what they believe students want to see when it truly isn't who they are. This is a mistake. Be yourself. For one thing, students can see right through the attempt. If they sense that you are not authentic, they will decide they can't trust you and a positive relationship won't develop. Students need to know they can be who they are and that "who they are" will be respected and valued and defended if it is ridiculed. That is what builds community. In the introductory vignette, Mrs. Sellers, through her verbal and nonverbal communication, made Lydia feel that she believed Lydia's family structure was not "appropriate." She did not allow for Lydia to bring her full self into the learning space. Lydia experienced harm, so now the question is, how does Mrs. Sellers repair the harm she caused? We will address that question in the "Restore" section later in this chapter.

Ways to Build, Maintain, and Restore Teacher-to-Student Relationships

Building, maintaining, and restoring the teacher-to-student relationship must be a fully intentional effort. This relationship is important throughout the school year and should be reflected on and fostered every day. Remember, your students are the main reason why you got into education in the first place. Taking time to build, maintain, and restore positive relationships with students is crucial.

Build

Building strong relationships can begin even before students step into your classroom. Intentionally setting the goal of building connections that can develop into strong relationships is a good starting point. Some examples of connections you can make before the start of school include calling to introduce yourself to the student or sending an introductory postcard (see the example in Figure 3.1). Doing either of these two things allows students to see, through your actions, that you care about them and the teacher-to-student relationship. It builds the foundation. Students are able to see that you are excited about the upcoming school year and that you value them—even before you step into the building. You are constructing a sense of psychological safety

FIGURE 3.1

Sample Introductory Postcard

Dear _____,

    I am so excited that you will be a part of our classroom community for the upcoming school year. Having you as part of this classroom will help our classroom to thrive together. I cannot wait to see all the amazing gifts you have and to see you shine this school year. See you on August 15!

Be well,

Mrs. Singleton

even before the students arrive in the classroom. This sense can lessen any nervousness and possible anxiety about the school year and about you as the teacher.

Taking this simple step to make a connection is the first brick laid in the foundation for building a strong teacher-student relationship. The following are some additional ideas.

Let students tell you their story. Regardless of grade level, Show and Tell never gets old. Giving students the opportunity to tell their story, to talk about themselves and their family, enables us to learn so much about them. If the term "Show and Tell" is too childish, try an activity called "Bringing Yourself in a Bag." This activity usually requires a person to bring four or five items that can fit into a bag and that symbolize who they are. For example, Nita's bag would hold a picture of family, a favorite book, a yoga mat, a Bible, and a journal. Mike's would contain a picture of family, a favorite pair of sneakers, an Apple Watch (for fitness tracking), a gift card for a massage, and his music.

The introductory example from Mrs. Sellers's classroom demonstrates that, although the activity is a great way to get to know students, it is imperative that teachers be self-aware enough to know what kinds of things may trigger a negative reaction and uproot biases they may not acknowledge. Once aware of these biases, teachers must do the necessary work to dismantle them. Such work likely will involve learning about different cultures and identities and growing in acceptance.

Practice active listening. Actually listening to what students want out of the classroom experience and how they want to learn is a way to show that you value them as learners in the classroom community. Feeling valued and heard contributes to students' willingness to build a positive relationship. Making the effort to do this is essential to the building stage of the relationship. Here are some ways to listen and get to know your students:

- Hold classroom meetings to discuss how your students learn best. Younger students can be involved in these discussions by showing them examples and pictures.

- Give surveys to your students asking them about how they learn and their expectations of their teacher.
- Have one-on-one chats with students at the beginning of the year. Doing so helps to open the door to a positive relationship.
- Create space in your teaching that allows for discussion and connection, which will allow you to get to know your students as both learners and humans.
- Have students create an identity poem. Working with a structure such as an "I Am" or a "Where I'm From" poem, students can describe their culture, background, experiences growing up, and likes and dislikes. Activities such as this allow teachers to get to know their students in a fun but authentic way.

Work together to set expectations. Setting expectations *with* students instead of doing so *for* them on your own will help your entire learning community. All relationships need clear communication on what is expected. The important thing for the teacher-to-student relationship is to create these expectations in community, together, through dialogue. A key point in this effort is making sure that students feel safe enough to be transparent. Ideally, every student should contribute to the conversation about expectations of students—and of teachers as well. It is equally important for teachers to be able to facilitate this discussion with an open mind and open heart.

Expectations for both students and teachers are important in building positive relationships because they help to construct a foundation of respect, with meaning that the parties have constructed together. Respect can mean different things to different people, so coming together to create a shared understanding is important. Figure 3.2 is a chart that you can use when thinking about creating expectations with students in community.

Maintain

Maintaining a positive teacher-to-student relationship is just as important as the building phase. This phase is where the most work lies, because it includes that intentionality we discussed earlier in the

FIGURE 3.2

Before, During, and After Steps in Creating Expectations with Students

Before	During	After
• Reflect on what you expect from the students in your classroom. • Think about each portion of your classroom—each part of your day. What do you want it to look like? • What are some things/areas/parts of your teaching day that demonstrate expectations on your part that are more flexible? • What are some ways that you can include students in the creation of the expectations that are more collaborative?	• During the creation of these expectations, begin with the question, What are some things that you expect of me as your teacher? Have some discussion around this point. Take time to listen to your students and have an open mind. Think about what you can agree with or add to the list. • Have students think about what expectations they should have as the learners in this community and discuss their ideas. This is a good time to really let students have an open, respectful dialogue. Together, come up with a list that everyone can agree on.	• Continue to review the expectations that were created for you as the educator and for your students. Review the expectations together in community daily, weekly, or monthly. • Continue to reflect on the expectations throughout the year, and alter as needed for the well-being of the community.

chapter. Here are some suggestions for how to maintain relationships with your students.

Check in and reflect. It should come as no surprise that maintaining good relationships with students is going to be critical throughout the year. Doing so requires continuously checking in, reflecting, and having open dialogue as to what is working or not working in your learning community. As the teacher, you must be the facilitator of these conversations, whether they are conducted in community or one-on-one. Working from the belief that conversations such as these are the foundation of good teaching and learning, you should ensure that these chats reaffirm the goal of a positive relationship where all parties feel safe, respected, valued, and listened to. Then and only then will checking in and reflecting be beneficial and have an impact.

Collaborate with other teachers. Collaborating with other teachers can give you insights or ideas for ways you can continue to build positive relationships with students in your classroom and with students beyond your four classroom walls. Discussions with other teachers can make you aware of the positive things their students are doing. You can also ask them for suggestions if you are struggling to build a relationship with a particular student in your classroom—especially if those teachers have that same student in their room. Building that collaboration can create a community around students to help them to thrive in school. Collaborating with other teachers builds a community outside of your classroom. It begins to build a relationship culture that extends throughout the school.

Dedicate time. We know that you are chuckling to yourself about this suggestion, because teachers are always "dedicating their time." But what we mean here is taking a deliberate moment to connect with your students' interests and discover things that may help you to keep your class interesting for them. You may be able to do this for a few minutes during class or during lunch. Whatever approach you use, be assured that teacher-to-student connection time is invaluable.

Restore

Sometimes an action or event happens that results in your teacher-to-student relationship taking a hit. It could be a negative classroom experience; it could be a misunderstanding or a miscommunication. In any case, restoration of the relationship has to take place.

Once again, let's think back to the vignette that introduced this chapter. Clearly Mrs. Sellers needs to begin to restore her relationship with Lydia. One way she can do that is by taking time with Lydia, one on one, to discuss what made her upset and to apologize for her action in making Lydia feel as though her family structure was wrong. Another step in making things right would be to allow Lydia the choice to reshare her bag with the class. This option is important because it would reveal whether she would feel safe or unsafe in doing so. If she doesn't feel safe, be willing to reiterate remorse and ask Lydia what she needs to feel safe and supported.

One thing to note here is that restoration takes time. Try not to allow that reality to deter you from trying. We want to also point out that the need for restoration, at times, may not be your fault. It may be something the student did or didn't do. However, please remember that as the teacher, you are the adult in the classroom. It's up to you to initiate the restoration process.

Whatever the circumstances, remember that the greater good is restoring the relationship so that students can thrive. The following are some suggestions for restoring a broken relationship.

Have a one-on-one conversation. Take time to have an authentic and open conversation with the student or students involved. During that conversation, be transparent and keep an open mind and an open heart. This recommendation means being an active, willing, and engaged listener. Bringing that mindset to the conversation may be challenging, but it is important for the rebuilding and restoring process to take place.

Don't be afraid to apologize. Hearing a teacher say the words "I'm sorry" shocks students because it allows them to see the adults as humans who make mistakes. Taking the time to apologize for wrongdoing is a game changer, but only if it is a genuine apology and rooted in the desire to grow and restore the relationship.

Collaborate with a student's family. Family members may know how to connect with students in order to restore a relationship and may help to expedite the restoration process as well. If it is OK with the student, take time to contact families in your effort to repair the relationship. Doing so can also help to build the teacher-to-family relationship, which we talk about in the next chapter.

* * *

Figure 3.3 highlights the main points related to building, maintaining, and restoring the teacher-to-student relationship. You can use it as a guide and reminder of ways to ensure your efforts are on the right path.

FIGURE 3.3

Ways to Build, Maintain, and Restore Teacher-to-Student Relationships

Build	Maintain	Restore
• Be authentically yourself. • Allow students to be authentically themselves. • Let students tell their story; ask questions. • Check in with students. • Try not to take things personally. • Be an active listener. • Be a learner about your students. • Identify common interests. • Create expectations of the community. • Set boundaries together with students. • Be available.	• Continue to follow through with expectations. • Check in with students (1:1 meetings). • Collaborate and discuss with other teachers to maintain the relationship with the student (connections, building on other relationships). • Continue to try not to take things personally. • Continue to be available for students. • Be consistent. • Reevaluate expectations.	• Be transparent. • Don't be afraid to apologize when necessary. • Allow space for openness and realness. • Continue to try not to take things personally. • Continue to check in with students (1:1 meetings). • Collaborate with other teachers/staff to aid in restoration. • Collaborate with families. • Review expectations.

SPEAKING FROM EXPERIENCE:

Observations from Michael and Nita

Michael's Observations

I was a licensed therapist before entering the school system, and I continue to be one. I start with this statement because I feel that my experience working with students vastly supersedes my time in the school building. I've worked with children, in some capacity, since I was a teenager and realize that the students themselves are what keep me coming back and working in the profession. Beginning during my first year in graduate school, I worked at a psychiatric residential treatment facility for children and adolescents. During my two years there, I learned the power of the follow-up conversation. The follow-up was reserved for those moments that required physical intervention that could lead to a therapeutic restraint and immediate or emergency use of an antipsychotic psychotropic. Due to the nature of the interaction, it was recommended and taught that a debriefing conversation should occur after the incident. This conversation helped prevent trauma and often deepened the relationship.

Similarly, follow-ups can make or break a relationship with students. I recall a specific encounter, years ago, when I was called to a classroom because a student was refusing to follow class rules and disrupting the classroom. Unfortunately, I had to assist with removal from the classroom. The student was livid! "How could you help *them?*" he asked. I sat down on the floor with him outside the classroom. I offered to process what happened with him, but all he could say was, "You were part of *them!* You're supposed to be my counselor, and counselors don't do none of what you just did." As I explained why everything just happened the way it did, he sat silently before saying, "I'm glad somebody could explain it to me 'cause people just be doing and saying whatever they want and expect you to get over it."

In that moment, it wasn't about some new innovative technique to engage students or a specific approach; it was a simple follow-up. When we're in the trenches and times are a little tough, it's those follow-ups with students that build more meaningful relationships. I wish I could say that student never had an issue again, but he did. However, I had far fewer incidents with him moving forward.

Nita's Observations

Student relationships are so important to me. When I think about all the students I have taught over my 13 years in the classroom and my later years as an instructional coach, I hope that I have poured into them the way they poured into me. I think about the students graduating. I think about the email sent to me from a former student wanting to grab coffee with his 5th grade teacher—me. I often think about how my students are doing. I think, hopefully, about how maybe one year of learning with me affected them in a positive way—through the relationship we built.

Many times throughout my career, there were students who had me wondering if I was connecting with them. I couldn't tell if I was getting through or having an impact. Now that I am 18 years into this work, I realize that most of the time you may not see the impact right away; but if you continue to pour into students, to cultivate the relationships and feed into them, you will have an impact. I often hear from former students' parents who have become friends via Facebook or email saying how much impact I have had. It brings me joy to see the kiddos I taught growing into young adults. When I see them, I pray that something I did—even a little bit of something—may have helped them along the way. I think about the greatest things that I did to foster our relationship. It was seeing them as a person, a human being. It was knowing and believing that respect goes both ways. It was listening to them and truly valuing them and what they had to say, even in 1st and 2nd grade. It was learning who they are. It was giving them a voice. All of those things I did as a teacher in order to foster relationships were things I did to build a "family"—a community in our learning space. That community—that family—was built on love, trust, respect, authenticity, and openness.

Reflective Questions

- How do you build relationships with your students?
- Can you identify your own biases toward students? How do you work through those biases?
- Can you recall a time when you had to restore a teacher-to-student relationship? What steps did you take to restore that relationship? What was the outcome? Is there anything you would have done differently?

- Ten years from now, what do you want your students to remember about you?

4 Teacher-to-Family Relationships

During her lunch break, Mrs. Brunswell is calling Eli's mother, Ms. Thompkins, for the fifth time this week about Eli's behavior. She gets no answer—again. She doesn't quite understand why his mother is not returning her calls. Eli has been acting up all week in class. He's been throwing paper across the room, falling out of his seat on purpose, picking arguments with other students, and spending a huge amount of time lingering in the bathroom. Mrs. Brunswell has no idea what Eli's problem is, but she knows she won't put up with it in her classroom. The first time she called, Eli's mother said that she would talk to him about his behavior. Clearly, she hasn't, because nothing has changed.

Mrs. Brunswell can't understand why parents don't just make their kids act right. When she was in school, she knew not to act up in class. The kids in her classroom just don't know discipline, and the parents—better to not even start on the parents. They must not care. They just send their kids to school and let the teachers deal with them, like babysitters.

Later that day, the school counselor pulls Mrs. Brunswell out of class and tells her that Eli and his mother have been living out of their car for the past three weeks because Ms. Thompkins lost her job two months ago. Mrs. Brunswell feels awful for not knowing this information and even worse that Ms. Thompkins didn't feel comfortable telling her this when she called the first time this week.

Why Teacher-to-Family Relationships Are Important

From the time they are born until the time they come to school, children have learned an immense amount of information and innumerable skills. They have learned how to speak, eat, and walk. They have learned about their family environment, what it looks like, who is a part of it, and how it's run. They have been taught all of these things even before stepping through the door of their first classroom. In short, the home is a child's first teacher.

We have no control over what students are taught during these earliest years of learning. However, once they walk through our classroom doors, we enter into the learning process that once solely belonged to each child's family. We are entering as an "added teacher" to the lives of our students. As the newest member of this teaching team, we have a responsibility to forge and build a relationship with each child's family. This relationship should center around respect, partnership, and commitment to the overall success of our students.

It is important to recognize that the teacher-to-family relationship is essential to the growth and well-being of our students. Without a positive relationship, the experience of all parties involved can be challenging, which is not what we desire. We desire the growth of the student we care about. We desire a partnership so that we can support each other and work together toward the ultimate success of students. No one goes in wanting to have a stressful and tense teacher-to-family relationship. No one goes in thinking that *not* having a relationship is better for the child.

An established and positive teacher-to-family relationship leads to continuity and consistency between school and home. That forged partnership can increase parental involvement and reduce truancy issues (Knopf & Swick, 2007).

At the same time, teachers should not pry or force themselves into the homes of their students. This relationship must develop and progress naturally. We must always remember that "parents deserve to be treated with consideration and deference. We need to lead with empathy and understanding when issues come to light" (Olender et al.,

2010, p. 60). To do that, a relationship must be built from the beginning of the student's experience in your classroom—or even before the start of school. Families must see you, the teacher, as a connector, a bridge, a builder. They must see you as a positive force in the life of their child, someone who wants that child to thrive in your classroom.

As with other relationships, trust and authenticity are key to building, maintaining, and restoring the teacher-to-family relationship. Let's examine each of these more closely within this context.

Trust

It is important to trust that a child's parents/caregivers are doing what they believe is best—the best that they know how to do. It becomes a slippery slope when we as educators get into a judgment zone of what should or shouldn't be happening in the home. We must trust that our families love their children, want what they believe is best for them, and want them to thrive in our classroom.

Trust works both ways, of course; and it's important to gain families' trust in *us*. With this in mind, building trust requires that we make sure that families know that we believe in their love for their child by expressing that belief verbally. This can occur at the beginning of the year, during a phone call, or at a conference with a family member. Acknowledging families' love for their child tends to minimize their distrust of the school system, facilitate collaboration, and help build the teacher-to-family relationship.

Authenticity

When building the teacher-to-family relationship, it is important to make sure the parents/caregivers know that the effort comes from an authentic place. Families often can tell when words are disingenuous. It is also important to note that being your authentic self does not mean you should avoid setting boundaries for families' involvement. You need to ensure that you continue to take care of yourself. For example, it is OK to decline an invitation to attend a student event outside of contracted work hours. After hours of work, sometimes the best thing to do is decompress in the comfort of your own home.

Family Diversity and the Importance of Inclusivity

Our world is diverse, and family structures show just how diverse our world actually is. The traditional nuclear family is not the norm as it once was in society. Children are a part of households of single parents, same-sex parents, families that have blended together, and so on. What you define as a family structure and what others define as a family structure may look and sound different; the definition is often quite subjective. What is not subjective is the love that is there regardless of what the family structure looks like. Remember, the family is a child's first teacher. You are an addition to that. You must respect the families you work with—period. This is not to say that the family should not demonstrate the same respect toward you. However, it is up to you to continuously build a bridge between home and school, and to extend an olive branch, if necessary. Communicate with an open mind and open heart, making sure that the student's family knows that you are there to support and respect them and their child. "Ultimately, it's about building a strong partnership with your families. Just as with any healthy relationship between two people, trust is a must for a successful partnership between groups. And a responsive relationship that respects cultural differences lays the foundation to build just that" (Shaikh, n.d.).

It is essential to ensure that we make students and their families feel welcome and included in the work we do with them each day. As stated earlier, doing so is important to the success of the whole child. This means that we may have work—"heart work"—to do in order to genuinely be inclusive. We may need to check our own personal biases of what a family can be and what that looks like. We must do that work so that we can offer the gift of inclusivity to our students so that they, too, can be open-minded in seeing and honoring family differences as well as similarities. Succeeding in this effort allows our students and their families to feel not only welcomed and included but also *seen*. Inclusivity enables everyone to become part of a school community coming together to help students thrive.

Ways to Build, Maintain, and Restore Teacher-to-Family Relationships

To understand the importance of teacher-to-family relationships, consider the situation described in the introductory vignette about Mrs. Brunswell and her relationship with Eli's mother, Ms. Thompkins. That relationship was not where Mrs. Brunswell wanted it to be. She held negative views about Ms. Thompkins without knowing the background story. She hadn't taken the time to build a relationship with Eli's mother and consequently was not aware that Eli was experiencing homelessness. If she had built a bridge at the beginning of the year, she may have known that the family was in crisis and been able to help Eli through it.

Build

Building the teacher-to-family relationship can involve a variety of strategies. Here are some ideas.

Look at the class roster without preconceptions. Every year, teachers receive a class roster. For many, the class roster sets the stage for the type of year teachers anticipate they will have. As you're reading this, you know exactly what we are referring to. Once you take a look at those names, your wheels start spinning; you remember hearing the names of the students who are exceptional—exceptionally good as well as exceptionally challenging, right? It doesn't matter what grade you teach; the class roster is always a subject of conversation among teachers. It shouldn't be, but it is. Teachers want to give the student's next teacher a "heads up" about what types of behaviors to expect.

Instead of listening to the negative views, nip the conversation in the bud. Do not allow another teacher's negative feelings from the previous year feed into your thoughts about the new year that lies ahead for you and your students. You both deserve to start fresh and begin the year on a high note. Whether a student and a particular teacher did not click the previous year has no bearing on the upcoming year or your connection with that student. That connection is up to you. It is up to you to start the year on a high note and to let all your students know that they have a fresh start.

Use a family communication checklist. Communicating effectively with families from the start of the school year will be important in building trusting, authentic relationships with them. Figure 4.1 is a checklist that you can use to ensure that you maintain the habit of intentional and constant communication throughout the school year.

FIGURE 4.1

Family Communication Checklist

Teacher: _____ Year: _____

Student: _____ Grade: _____

Time Period	Form of Communication	Notes
Beginning of the year	☐ Reach out to families via a phone call to introduce yourself and welcome your students to your class. ☐ Send an introductory email introducing yourself to your families and providing important information about the beginning of the year. ☐ Send a postcard or a written note to your students to extend the welcome even further. ☐ Send home weekly/monthly newsletters to keep families abreast of what is happening in class. ☐ Prepare for parent (or caregiver)/teacher/student conferences. If you notice a decline in grades or change in behavior before the conference, let parents/caregivers know ahead of time to avoid blindsiding them. ☐ Call home as needed. Err on the side of overcommunicating versus not communicating at all.	
Middle of the year (before the winter break)	☐ Call home for a family check-in. ☐ Conduct conferences with students you are concerned about. ☐ Send home weekly or monthly newsletters to keep families abreast of what is happening in class. ☐ Call home as needed. Err on the side of overcommunicating versus not communicating at all.	

(continued)

FIGURE 4.1—(*continued*)

Family Communication Checklist

Time Period	Form of Communication	Notes
End of the year	☐ Conduct conferences for students who you are concerned about. ☐ Send home weekly or monthly newsletters to keep families abreast of what is happening in class and to provide end-of-the-year information. ☐ Call home as needed. Err on the side of overcommunicating versus not communicating at all. ☐ Send home a positive note about the student's strengths and why you enjoyed having the student in your classroom.	

Implement a positive intervention plan (PIP). Implementing a positive intervention plan is one strategy that would have improved Mrs. Brunswell's ability to help Eli. It could have helped her to be more intentional about reaching out to Eli's family (and the families of all the other students in her class) and build a bridge. The PIP is a plan of intentional action, a purposeful effort that helps to build positive, productive relationships. It is a go-to plan to make sure that you, as the teacher, are taking the initiative and staying the course in relationship building with families. The PIP allows you to check in throughout the year to make sure that you are following through on your intention to connect.

Figure 4.2 (see pp. 56–57) shows sample PIPs for elementary schools and for middle and high schools. They can be adapted to fit the needs of any school or district. The forms include some of the suggestions that appear in the family communication checklist, along with spaces where teachers can log whatever positive interactions they make with families and ideas for building connections throughout the year, such as inviting families to class events. (The "FAB forms" shown in the sample PIPs are ways to highlight positive behavior. We describe them in more detail later in this chapter.)

Maintain

Maintaining a relationship with families and caregivers is going to be essential as you move throughout the school year. We want families with us on the journey of success for their students. It is important that we are consistent in our communications and are including them often in the journey. Here are some ways to do that.

Continue to implement a PIP. In addition to its usefulness in building relationships, the PIP helps in maintaining them, providing teachers with reminders to continue to intentionally connect with families. Notice that the sample shown in Figure 4.2 includes specific suggestions for reaching out at all points in the school year—beginning, middle, and end.

Be consistent in communicating. Communication is how we build and maintain the connections that lead to productive relationships. To succeed in the effort, communication has to be consistent, and consistency requires time.

Now, we already know what you're thinking. How can consistent communication happen when you have to teach, give assessments, be a part of school committees, and so much more? On top of everything else, how can you find the time for consistent communication? Here's the thing: that time is critical to the well-being of students—to their growth and academic success. They are unlikely to thrive without the support of strong teacher-to-family relationships, and consistent communication is the pathway to building and maintaining those relationships. Although it may seem like a lot of work initially, it is some of the best work you can do as an educator.

Once again, the positive intervention plan can be a helpful tool. In addition to its usefulness in fostering intentionality in your relationship with families, it ensures consistency. If you take the time to *intentionally* and *consistently* communicate with families, using the PIP's suggestions for making phone calls, sending emails, sharing positive feedback, and other actions, you are much more likely to succeed in maintaining the strong ties you have worked so hard to build.

Spread good news via the Fantastically Amazing Behavior (FAB) form. The FAB form, shown in Figure 4.3 (see p. 58), is a way to highlight a student's good behavior. It can help educators to

FIGURE 4.2

Positive Intervention Plans (PIPs) for Elementary and Middle/High School Levels

ELEMENTARY SCHOOL LEVEL

Teacher: _____ Grade: _____ Year: _____

Time Period	Positive Action Taken	Notes
Before the first day of school	☐ Reach out to families via phone call to introduce yourself and welcome your students to your class. ☐ Send a postcard or a note to your students to extend the welcome even further.	
Beginning of the year (after the first few weeks of school)	☐ Send home a FAB form to share a positive behavior that you noticed. ☐ Follow up with a phone call or an email about the FAB form.	
Date:	Positive action(s):	
Date:	Positive action(s):	
Middle of the year (before the winter break)	☐ Call home or send an email to every family relating something positive their student did. ☐ Double up the positive calls or notes for students who may have behavior challenges.	
Date:	Positive action(s):	
Date:	Positive action(s):	
End of the year	☐ Call home or send an email to every family relating something positive their student did. ☐ Double up the positive calls or notes for students who may have behavior challenges.	
Throughout the year	☐ Allow parents to come to the classroom to read books to the students. ☐ Invite parents to class events. ☐ Ask for at-school and at-home volunteers.	

MIDDLE/HIGH SCHOOL LEVEL

Teacher: _____ Grade: _____ Year: _____

Time Period	Positive Action Taken	Notes
Before the first day of school	☐ Reach out to families via email to introduce yourself, welcome your students to your class, and express your excitement about the upcoming year. This can be done via a mass email. ☐ Send a postcard or a note to your students to extend the welcome even further.	
Beginning of the year (after the first few weeks of school)	☐ Send home a FAB form to share a positive behavior that you noticed the student doing. The FAB form can be sent via email. ☐ Make a phone call or send an email to follow up with the FAB form.	
Date:	Positive action(s):	
Date:	Positive action(s):	
Middle of the year (before the winter break)	☐ Send home a FAB form to share a positive behavior that you noticed the student doing. The FAB form can be sent via email. ☐ Double up the positive calls or notes for students who may have behavior challenges or ones who may often get overlooked.	
Date:	Positive action(s):	
Date:	Positive action(s):	
End of the year	☐ Send a positive email to every family, including something positive their student did in class and what a joy it was to have the student in your classroom.	
Throughout the year	☐ Invite parents to class events. ☐ Invite parents to come in for Career Day. ☐ Ask for at-school and at-home volunteers.	

purposefully look for students' positive behavior and commend them for doing it. The behavior can be a gesture as small as giving another student a compliment, picking up trash from the floor, or inviting a fellow student to join a collaborative learning group. In terms of maintaining teacher-to-family relationships, encouraging students to share the FAB form with their families or sending it to them directly lets them know that you are intentional in seeing the good in every student.

FIGURE 4.3

Sample FAB (Fantastically Amazing Behavior) Form

Teacher: _____ Date: _____

Student: _____

FAB Displayed:
Why I thought this was so AMAZING:
Keep up the great work! Allgood Elementary School is so proud of you!

Often we look at behavior through a negative lens—things that students do that are not acceptable. However, studies have shown that highlighting positive behavior in one student breeds additional positive behavior in that student and in others (Law et al., 2012). The FAB form can be one way to foster that tendency.

Sometimes an incentive or a reward can encourage the behavior that is celebrated in the FAB form. Elementary-age students may enjoy getting candy, ice cream, or popcorn; and a pizza party can be a reward for a whole-class effort. Many middle and high school students would prefer a "no homework" pass or free time in class.

Some people may think that rewarding students is a form of bribery. However, incentives are not unheard of in workplaces. How is that different from highlighting the great behavior students are showing in the classroom?

Restore

Sometimes, relationships with families have to be restored. The underlying issue or problem could be a misunderstanding or miscommunication. Or it might have occurred before the school year and have nothing to do with the current teacher. However, to ensure students' families are part of this journey, we have to take time to slow down and restore the relationship. Here are some suggestions to begin the restoration process.

Have the hard conversations. No one signs up for this part of the job. As educators, we love to create magic in our classrooms, to ignite the spark that brightens up the day for our students. However, when it comes to problematic behaviors, we can name the behaviors and even think of solutions, but that "family conversation" piece is a challenge. Many of us wonder about or struggle with how to connect with parents, and we experience various emotions at the prospect of having those hard conversations.

Before and during the conversation, consider two factors: (1) your relationship with the student's family and (2) your student's relationship with the family. Both factors can significantly affect the course and outcome of the meeting. As educators, we have more leeway to engage in candid conversations regarding students' academic performance or behavior when we have developed amicable relationships with our students' families. Additionally, when we are aware of relationship issues between our students and their families, we have a tendency to soften our approach, almost in an attempt to protect the feelings of the student and to prevent collateral relational damage.

Let's take a moment to consider the following "Hard Conversations Checklist," which can make the prospect of discussing difficult issues with parents a little less daunting:

1. **Prepare.** Address those anxious feelings. Name them and move on to identifying how you will handle unforeseen circumstances. How will you convey information if the parent or caregiver becomes defensive? Remember, most verbal attacks on educators are more about frustration over struggles students may be experiencing and not always a personal attack on you as the professional. If issues relate to the quality of the student's work, have actual examples available for reference. And here's a tip: always have more positive examples than negative examples. Every student does something well. It's up to you as the educator to catch students behaving or performing well. Those positive examples help you prepare your "sandwich." Parents almost always prefer their sandwiches in this form: POSITIVE–negative/problematic–POSITIVE. Solutions can be easier to find after you serve the sandwich.

2. **Set the tone.** Consider your tone and choose your words carefully. Your words have meaning and significant impact. Optimism and pessimism are easily conveyed in vocal tone; let optimism lead the way. Start the meeting by reiterating the purpose: Why are we here today? Then start to serve your sandwich (POSITIVE–negative/problematic–POSITIVE).

3. **Encourage collaboration.** Every parent or caregiver believes they are an expert on their child. Don't dismiss this opportunity to collaborate. There may be a potential strategy, approach, or phrase that you are unaware of and that will produce the desired change in behavior. Guess who may know that strategy, approach, or phrase? Yup, the family. Take every opportunity to encourage a collaborative partnership with families.

4. **Maintain composure.** Not all hard conversations end with a productive plan of action. Some will leave you needing a timeout with your favorite adult beverage. Regardless of what is said, your obligation to yourself and your profession suggests you should not resort to losing your composure or taking cheap shots at families. Yes, even the gold-star teachers have a breaking point. What can you say when your buttons have been pushed more than a TV remote control by a toddler?

Looking at it from a "restore" point of view, let's revisit the vignette from the beginning of the chapter. Because Eli's mom is no longer answering calls, Mrs. Brunswell decides to send an email, but what is she going to say? How can she address her concerns but convey the level of empathy and understanding needed to foster change? One possibility is the sample email shown in Figure 4.4.

FIGURE 4.4

Sample Email

Greetings, Ms. Thompkins:

I just wanted to reach out to you regarding Eli. He's typically been a big helper in my class and so nice to his classmates. Unfortunately, he's had a hard time lately. Eli has thrown paper across the room, fallen out of his seat on purpose, started arguments with other students, and spent a huge amount of time lingering in the bathroom. This just doesn't seem like him, and I was hoping that you and I could help Eli work through whatever may be causing this recent change in behavior. I would love to speak with you to further discuss. If necessary, we have many resources that may be beneficial. Please let me know how we can best help Eli return to being my big helper and the leader I know him to be.

What happens next? Does this email magically motivate Ms. Thompkins to contact Ms. Brunswell? In a perfect world, this communication would make everything OK, and Ms. Thompkins would immediately jump onboard. However, emails of this sort may fall on deaf ears and not because the parent or caregiver doesn't care but because the needs of the parent or family are of greater importance than the problematic behavior exhibited in your classroom. Even though we complete all the steps and go through all the proper channels, that collaborative partnership we so desire with our students' families may not happen... and that's alright. Because we are professional educators, we will undoubtedly continue to strive to develop that collaborative partnership. Part of the continued striving includes walking families through next steps, even when the steps are difficult and conversations are hard, and even when we may have to acknowledge the part we played in a particular situation as well.

* * *

Figure 4.5 highlights the main points related to building, maintaining, and restoring the teacher-to-family relationship. You can use it as a guide and reminder of ways to ensure your efforts are on the right path.

FIGURE 4.5

Ways to Build, Maintain, and Restore Teacher-to-Family Relationships

Build	Maintain	Restore
• Use the family communication checklist (Figure 4.1). • Complete a PIP (Figure 4.2) to aid in fostering an initial relationship. • Have the student or family member complete a "getting-to-know-you" form. • Intentionally spend time with students (e.g., meet as a "lunch bunch" once a week).	• Use FAB form (Figure 4.3) to highlight positive behavior. • Conduct class meetings first thing in the morning. • Continue to meet with your lunch bunch. • Continue to complete PIPs to maintain ties with families. • Make yourself available (e.g., have social-emotional check-ins with students during class work time).	• Identify the issue. • Prepare to restore what's broken; be ready to acknowledge personal fault if pertinent. • Confront the challenge; have the difficult conversation. • Schedule a meeting with families to begin or continue the restoration process. • Send notes home with the student to clarify and communicate.

SPEAKING FROM EXPERIENCE:
Observations from Michael and Nita

Michael's Observations

I still remember it like it was yesterday—my first invitation to an SST (Student Support Team) meeting. I wasn't quite an educator yet, but I was the therapist working with the 4th grade student who was the focus of the meeting. As I sat at the table awaiting the introduction of all the stakeholders, I realized two things: the vibe in the room was tense, and the teacher-parent relationship was not good. The parent and the teacher exchanged looks of disgust and contempt. After the introductions, the teacher reiterated the purpose of the meeting and stated, "We're all here to help Jacob get back on track; but remember, he has to want it for himself." I sat there thinking, "Oh boy! She really didn't need to add that last part." Why? "Remember, he has to want it for himself" may be a true statement, but it definitely does *not* set the tone you want at the beginning of a meeting, especially when two of the participants appear to be adversaries.

As the meeting continued, Jacob's mother repeatedly interrupted the teacher and minimized disruptive behaviors described by other participants. Finally, Jacob's teacher muttered, "Know where he gets it from now." Jacob's mother stood up and demanded that the teacher repeat herself, stating, "Say it again, you bold... I'm 'bout to show you what else he got from me!" I interjected and convinced Jacob's mother to speak to me in the hallway, outside the meeting. Once de-escalated, the meeting continued, and everyone began to discuss possible interventions, which led to further discussion about some of the things Jacob was doing well. After some time and eventual collaboration, the meeting ended with a plan for moving forward. However, how much damage was done to the teacher-family relationship? Could that relationship be repaired? If so, how?

Nita's Observations

It's so telling how a positive relationship becomes damaged in a matter of minutes. The wrong statement, the wrong tone, a lack of communication—any of these can break down what was once a positive relationship or get in the way of creating one in the first place.

I remember being a classroom teacher when I suspected that one of my young students was being abused by her uncle. I did all the things I needed to do to comply with the protocol; however, the delicacy of the situation and the parents' denial led to an unfortunate outcome. They didn't want to believe what my student told me when I shared the information with them—and they were angry. I took their anger personally. I made the situation about me and not about the parents and my student. Instead of making the student the heart of the relationship with the parents, I made it about the parents not believing me. I made it about me being right versus making sure, above all, that the student was safe and well.

My principal had to pull me aside, and I was actually removed from the meetings with the parents because I was no longer the bridge needed to help my student. I severed that bridge as I allowed my anger to flow. In the end, my student was removed from my classroom and placed into another teacher's class.

This experience was painful, but I learned so much from it. The removal of the student from my class was the right decision. I was hurt and I was angry, but neither one of those emotions was in the best interest of the student. I learned that it's important to build bridges instead of burning them. I learned that every action can either build up or break down a positive relationship with families. We want to ensure that the actions we take are ones that build the bridge.

Reflective Questions

- How do your personal biases of what a family "should be" interfere with building connections with your families?
- What are some strategies and approaches described in this chapter that you would like to implement, and why?
- How could the teacher described in Michael's observations have handled the meeting differently?
- What are some ways Nita could have built a bridge with the family when dealing with a delicate situation such as abuse?

5 ⛼ Teacher-to-Teacher Relationships

The school year was underway. Preplanning was in full swing, and teachers had been going from one meeting to another all day. Vice Principal Tatum was having an afternoon meeting with teachers to discuss a.m./p.m. duty. This gathering usually focused on the importance of meeting and greeting students as they enter and exit the school building. However, Ms. Henry had decided to air her grievances with colleagues during the Questions & Concerns portion of the meeting. Immediately after Vice Principal Tatum opened the floor for questions, Ms. Henry stated, "What's our liability?" VP Tatum appeared confused before responding, "Umm... what do you mean?" Ms. Henry went on to suggest that there were not enough people assigned to a particular area of the building. She stated, "I know people who are assigned but never show up. What's the liability for the people that are actually showing up and doing the responsible thing? What happens if a student gets hurt, and it's because Mrs. Davis and Mr. Samuels were not there to supervise the area? Are we penalized for our irresponsible colleagues that never show up?"

Three of Ms. Henry's colleagues sat silently, scowling but not at all surprised by her statements. Ms. Henry is known for this kind of behavior. She takes any opportunity to make herself look better than her colleagues at the expense of others. Ironically, she does not understand why other teachers often distance themselves from her and her antics.

Why Teacher-to-Teacher Relationships Are Important

Countless articles and research studies highlight the importance of teacher-to-student relationships and their measurable impact on the academic success of students. However, there is limited research highlighting the effect that teacher-to-teacher relationships have on overall teacher satisfaction, teacher morale, and teacher longevity, whether it be the amount of time a teacher spends in one school or the overall number of years spent in the profession.

We nevertheless ask you to take a moment to think about how any relationship, good or bad, affects us as humans. As educators, we're not immune to the effects of bad relationships with colleagues. Strikingly similar to the teacher-to-student relationship, the teacher-to-teacher relationship can also make or break our experience in the profession. As with many situations, when aspects of a relationship become toxic, we are more prone to leave than we are to stay to work it out. We would be remiss if we didn't acknowledge that there are some teachers who may hold the title of a teacher, but don't have their own classroom filled with students in the traditional sense. For example, many special education teachers may not have a homeroom and instead push into classrooms throughout the day in order to support students on their caseload. They are sometimes treated as an assistant when they are also a teacher in the classroom.

Teachers are reportedly more resilient and have a greater potential to thrive when they have good working relationships with other teachers in the school (Waddell, 2010). As simple as this sounds and as easy as some may think it is to create good working relationships, doing so can be challenging. Unlike the relationships teachers have with administrators or students, the teacher-to-teacher relationship is devoid of any inherent power differential. Although the teachers are on the same level playing field, they must share mutual respect for the working relationship to be successful.

Many of us have experienced instances when we've felt devalued, unappreciated, or taken for granted by a colleague. Conversely, we may have experienced the feeling of knowing that we are in the trenches with someone who respects and appreciates the work we do. Findings reveal that the quality of teachers' relationships with one another matters more than the number of ties they have (Hopkins et al., 2019). A key question we seek to answer, then, is, *How can we create and foster high-quality teacher-to-teacher relationships?* As we've seen with other relationships, trust and authenticity are key elements.

Trust

Building trust is crucial to fostering strong, productive teacher-to-teacher relationships. Teachers must know that they can rely on each other, that they are going to do what they said they would do. When thinking about what makes an ideal team of teachers, we think of teachers who are not in competition with one another; rather, they think about the good of the team and the students who are affected by the team. They put the good of the group ahead of the good of themselves as individuals. Doing so builds trust, contributing to the foundation of solid teacher-to-teacher relationships.

Authenticity

We have said it before and will say it again: being your authentic self is crucial to building, restoring, and maintaining any relationship, and the teacher-teacher relationship is no exception. It is important to know that folks are who they say they are. It is important to know that they present their authentic selves in all spaces. Teacher-to-teacher relationships thrive in this situation and become the best that they can be. Being authentic is good for both yourself and the relationship. Any attempt to dumb yourself down or shrink yourself to fit in is not beneficial to you or to your colleagues. Ironically, doing so may cause harm because of potential resentment and animus that develops within you or among others who sense your lack of authenticity. It's hard to hide the "true you" for an extended amount of time, regardless of the situation or environment.

Ways to Build, Maintain, and Restore Teacher-to-Teacher Relationships

Building, maintaining, and restoring teacher-to-teacher relationships happens when the people involved are open and unafraid of vulnerability, have mutual respect, and sincerely want to come together for the sake of their students. Coincidentally, these factors contribute to individual peace of mind and the overall morale of the school. It can happen. However, both parties must be open and willing to make the relationship work for the good of everyone involved.

Sometimes we forget the power of community when we are on our own island. We forget that people need other people in order to thrive. Working in the field of education is a better experience when we can engage with other teachers, learn from them, lead them, and laugh with them. The outcome is better for our students and better for ourselves. But often we wonder how we can get to this good place if there is tension within a team or department. How can we come together if the environment is characterized by a lack of cohesiveness, with everyone working on their own islands?

In discussing the importance of and the actions related to building, maintaining, and restoring relationships, we would be remiss if we did not discuss an unwritten rule among teachers, which is to avoid petty, unnecessary behaviors. These behaviors can often make or break the relationship at the outset. Examples include presenting a coworker's idea as if it were your own, running to the copy machine to get ahead of someone else, intentionally not sharing information with a colleague who was out sick, or purposely not speaking to another teacher in the hallway.

Among the many petty behaviors that can be named, one that is worth more discussion is "teacher tattling." What does that mean, you may wonder. Is this some type of unwritten rule of the educator world or some type of joke? Unfortunately it's neither, and it's common in schools everywhere. On any given day, if you listen closely, you will hear a story about how one teacher unnecessarily tattled on another. Teachers may do this in an effort to be viewed more favorably or put themselves in a better light, or because they feel like something is unfair or they are unhappy with their own situation. We're not talking about telling on another teacher because that teacher is doing harm to students or encouraging presumably negative behavior. Teacher tattling is more along the lines of telling on a fellow teacher who left the building five minutes early. This kind of seemingly mundane "telling on someone" can sour any teacher-to-teacher relationship, and it is imperative that educators understand the long-term effects it has not only on the relationship, but also on their own reputation and on teacher morale. In short, such petty behaviors are detrimental to all educators involved, ultimately undermining any attempt at developing a positive teacher-to-teacher relationship.

Build

Building productive teacher-to-teacher relationships affects many aspects of life in schools, and one of the most significant is the quality of teacher teams. It is important to acknowledge that building the relationship between a new teacher and an established veteran on the team can be particularly challenging and can lead to teamwide tension. Sometimes the tension arises because individuals essentially lack respect for each other. Mutual respect is going to be key in team building and making sure that everyone is thriving. This does not mean that everyone on the team has to be best friends, spending time together outside of school and texting throughout the evening. But it does mean that all team members must take time to paus. and reflect, to value each person's opinion and voice, to collaborate and share, and above all to communicate.

There are many ways to build productive teacher relationships at the outset. Here are some ways to approach this phase.

Get to know each other. Obviously, taking time to get to know each other is essential to building the teacher-to-teacher relationship. It's important to know what your fellow teachers' professional strengths and growth areas are. It is also important to get to know who the person is (more specifically, understanding their background, beliefs, and perspectives) and how they operate, for better or worse. When you know each other, you can begin to build the relationship that will aid in supporting students.

Be accountable for your job duties and responsibilities. This is a simple but important thing to remember: do your job. No one wants to have to do your job for you. However, being accountable means knowing all of what your job entails. Once you know exactly what your job involves and the related expectations, try to consistently do those things. We know well how life outside of work can interfere with being able to meet those expectations from time to time. Unforeseen events such as a death or an illness in the family, or a health issue you are confronting yourself, can disrupt your good intentions. Life happens. If you cannot perform an expected duty, let your team know; speak up. It is better to speak up and be open than to suffer in silence, leaving the work undone.

Communicate and be a listener. Take time to listen—really listen. Listen with your whole heart, not just your ears. Although the school building brings us together, don't limit your effort to school-related issues. When you have a colleague who trusts you enough to share personal information, specifically something that is affecting their life, pay attention. Being present not only helps build understanding, it also often strengthens the relationship. We have said it before, and we will say it again: communicate, communicate, communicate. Remember that communication takes many forms, both verbal and nonverbal. Take the time to slow down and give the gift of listening.

Maintain

Building the teacher-to-teacher relationship is work, but maintaining it is crucial. Like the building phase, the maintenance phase requires open communication and honesty. It requires ongoing collaboration and respect for each other's ideas even if those ideas are different from our own. It also requires being there for one another and acknowledging that we are human. There will be times when we need to be the shoulder for someone to cry on, the ears to vent to. We may even need to fill in the gap when one member of the team is having a crisis or an issue. Remember that although some may think of educators as superheroes, sometimes a superhero needs to put the cape on the shelf and be human. The strongest teams are the ones that allow vulnerability to seep through, that are open. When that happens, the effect can be powerful. A trust-filled group of teachers who are genuine is one in which each member thrives.

There are many ways to maintain positive, productive teacher-to-teacher relationships. Here are a few ideas to help you in this phase.

Continue to communicate. Sometimes our needs change. Some years can bring unforeseen student behavior issues, increased family responsibility at home, or an opportunity to further your own professional career. These are just a few examples of circumstances that may change our personal and professional needs. When that happens, it is important to share that information with those we are working with. We have to remember that our colleagues are not mind readers. They can't support us if they don't know about something that has affected our professional or personal life.

Check in and reflect as a team. If you are not already doing this, make it a point to periodically check in to see how every team member is doing individually and how the group is doing collectively. This "pulse check" is imperative for maintaining teacher-to-teacher relationships and allows individuals or the team as a whole to make necessary pivots. Obviously, an authentic conversation requires that the members of the group feel safe and trust one another. Some questions to ask might include the following:

- **How is everyone doing personally?** This question allows for connection but also can be important for how teachers feel when they show up at school. If they are comfortable enough with their teacher teams to open up, they are more likely to believe that their colleagues will support them in the workplace—and vice versa. They will be there for one another. Holding space for this question allows them to see each other as people first and teachers second.
- **How are we working together as a team?** Being honest in responding to this question makes room for praise, appreciation, and growth. Building and maintaining a strong team requires collectively assessing its strength, as well as identifying areas for improvement.

- **What are some amazing things we have done so far together?** When you focus on the positive things you have done as a team, you are drawing attention to what is going well and setting the stage for happy feelings in the future. Try to find at least one or two things that are amazing—no matter how small. Celebrate them.
- **What are some obstacles we have overcome as a team?** Thinking about the things that you have overcome builds team resilience. It is advisable to look at the broad picture of the team's work rather than focusing only on one or two things that may not be going well. Doing so helps to highlight the team's strength and problem-solving ability, giving members the impetus to continue to work on challenges.
- **What are some things we need to change?** Change doesn't necessarily have to be a bad thing. Introspection leading to change makes room for growth.

Connect outside the school building. Sometimes maintaining the team relationship and getting to know one another better involves time spent together outside the school building. This could be having lunch together on a workday or meeting after school or on a weekend for a painting class. Coming together in an out-of-school setting can help to keep the synergy alive among the team members.

Restore

As in all relationships, there will be times in the teacher-to-teacher relationship when you have to patch things up, have a difficult conversation, or even give space to another person when a problem or issue has arisen. Maybe a team member felt disrespected or ignored by the team. Whatever the reason, restoring a relationship is by far the most vulnerable—but necessary—part of the BMR process. The following suggestions are some ways to restore a damaged relationship.

Check in with yourself. Take time before digging into the issue or problem to check in with yourself. How are you feeling? What emotions are coming up when you think about the issue or problem?

Reflect on the problem or issue. Give the problem or issue some space and take some time to reflect. If journaling is something you like to do, that could be helpful. Think of how you might have handled the situation differently. Although taking time to reflect is important, don't overdo it. Recognize the need to move on to actively attempting to restore the relationship.

Have a conversation. Restoring begins with having a conversation with the other person or persons involved. The restoration conversation may mean humbling yourself, offering a metaphorical olive branch, and opening up the space for healthy healing. Enter this space with an open head and an open heart.

Restoration takes a good bit of humility, vulnerability, and an apologetic spirit if the situation calls for that. Sometimes it calls for a meeting of the minds. Restoration is not easy, but it is essential when we consider the ultimate goal of doing our best for our students.

* * *

Figure 5.1 highlights the main points related to building, maintaining, and restoring the teacher-to-teacher relationship. You can use it as a guide and reminder of ways to ensure your efforts are on the right path.

SPEAKING FROM EXPERIENCE:
Observations from Michael and Nita

Michael's Observations

I didn't enter education in the traditional way. I went to school to become a therapist, came to a fork in the road during my last year (deciding between a school setting or community mental health), and decided to choose a career in community mental health because it enabled me to complete my master's degree faster. By following the community mental health route, I was able to fine-tune my own relationship skills while helping others develop theirs.

Thank God I took the path that I did in terms of eventually becoming a professional school counselor. Although my time in community mental health gave me lots of experience working on teams and collaborating with colleagues, I did not have a lot of experience navigating the world of public education policy. Probably much like other professionals transitioning into education, I remember feeling like a fish out of water when teachers started speaking in school district–specific acronyms. This was all new to me. I had come from a supervisor position and felt inadequate in the early stages of entering the school system. To move past that inadequate feeling, I allowed myself to be a sponge and learn from others. That learning led me to build relationships. Had I not developed relationship skills through previous career experience, my transition would have been far more difficult.

I remember being transparent from day one. I didn't intentionally bare my insecurities, but I don't remember hiding them either. I never felt a need to be anyone other than myself, regardless of the situation. I recently asked my co-counselors (aka the "Counselor Crew") what they remembered most about my entry into the school system five years ago. Their answer still rings in my ear: "We knew you were always gonna be you, regardless." I think by me being authentically myself, my Counselor Crew knew that I was going to bring my years of earlier experience as a therapist into my work in the school system, regardless of the circumstances. The core of who I am remained unchanged.

I realize my experience is atypical, and I'm fortunate to have had such a pleasant transition. As I write this, I am still employed at the school where I started. It's been a blessing, because I've never felt like I was a burden to my co-counselors, even when I knew I was asking a million questions. There was never a time when I wasn't encouraged to grow or enabled to pursue additional endeavors. I've heard the horror stories and have experienced a few myself, but the Counselor Crew always had my back, and over the years we developed a synergy that remains today.

Nita's Observations

I absolutely love talking about teacher-to-teacher relationships because the topic always makes me think about the "Wolf Pack." I speak of this teacher team often because of just how well we flowed. The Wolf Pack began in 2008. When I came to the school, I had four years of experience behind me. Those four years made me feel confident as a teacher, but I was also entering a new school building and a four-person team that had already been established. I was the new person on campus.

At first, I lay low and followed the team. I got to know them, and they got to know me. Because the team was already established, I felt it was important to go along with the program for a while. From my perspective, it showed that I respected the work that they had been doing. It also showed that I realized that I was entering their territory. I was the newbie; I needed to take time to get to know how the school operated, the people in it, and where I fit.

As time went on, I began using my voice more and more. I began offering ideas and suggestions during team meetings. However, I was also open to new ideas, and I was a learner. In 2009, the team shifted a bit. The team leader moved to another school, and we added two new people. Getting to know them took time, and getting to know their strengths and areas of growth was equally important.

As I reflect on what made our team so great, I realize now that we built on each other's strengths. That is why it is important to know both strengths and areas of growth. We all fed into our strengths, and because of that, we were a well-oiled machine. We collaborated, we planned together, we shared, we communicated (even when we needed to have tough conversations), we were in it together, and we knew that being in it together made us stronger. We each had our jobs to do for the collective work of the team, but we also had our unique gifts as well. We had our sunshine person, our over-the-top person, our realistic person, our timekeeper, our leader, and our overthinker. But we realized, as much as we joked about each other's jobs, that each one was important. We valued and respected one another for what we knew, and when it was time to learn (even learn hard things), we were open.

That was the Wolf Pack. We still communicate to this day, and we know that the five years we were together were special. I want that Wolf Pack feeling to be the case for every teacher team I work with as a coach. I know that when the teachers work together as my Wolf Pack did, students thrive.

FIGURE 5.1

Ways to Build, Maintain, and Restore Teacher-to-Teacher Relationships

Build	Maintain	Restore
• Value one another's opinions. • Communicate. • Be a listener. • Collaborate with other teachers and your team members. • Be yourself. • Check in with your teachers/team members ("How are you doing?"). • Be mindful that it takes effort on both sides. • Be accountable for your job duties and responsibilities.	• Continue to communicate. • Continue to listen. • Continue to collaborate. • Continue to check in with one another. • Continue to be accountable for your duties and responsibilities. • Connect as a team. • Complete a team check-in.	• Communicate, communicate, communicate. • Be respectful. • Be an active listener, noting both verbal and nonverbal communication. • Be open. • Allow yourself to be vulnerable. • Make space for forgiveness.

Reflective Questions

- What are some ways you build relationships with teachers?
- How did your last hard conversation with a teacher colleague go?

- Describe characteristics of a team that you thought was a great group to work on. If you haven't had that experience yet, what characterizes your ideal teacher team?
- How would other teachers describe you? (Ask teachers for their view, but only do so when you are ready to receive honest feedback.)

6

Teacher-to-Administrator Relationships

Mrs. Towns has just completed her first semester as a 5th grade teacher. This is her first year in education, and the transition from student teaching to having her own classroom has been eventful. She is getting ready to meet with her assistant principal, Ms. Walker, to go over feedback from her last evaluation. Ms. Walker has felt stressed and overwhelmed due to a recent teacher shortage but understands the importance of connecting with her teachers. Mrs. Towns has felt anxious and concerned about her upcoming meeting with Ms. Walker and sure that classroom management and lack of rigor in lesson plans would be areas of concern.

As Mrs. Towns sat in front of Ms. Walker's desk, Ms. Walker invited her to move to a nearby table in her office. Ms. Walker began the meeting by acknowledging the effort and dedication Mrs. Towns exhibits in her classroom. She went on to mention specific areas where Mrs. Towns could grow, then encouraged her to share her view of her strengths and areas for growth. Ms. Walker also made sure to prompt Mrs. Towns periodically to determine feelings and thoughts related to the feedback. Ms. Walker reassured her new teacher that she was doing great things in the classroom and would continue to grow.

Later that afternoon, Mrs. Towns received a note in her school mailbox that said, "You may question yourself and your decisions a lot this first year. That's OK; we've all done it. Continue to grow personally and professionally, and always remember: You are an amazing educator and will change the lives of your students." Mrs. Towns smiled as she felt tears swelling in her eyes. The meeting went better than anticipated, but why? How?

Why Teacher-to-Administrator Relationships Are Important

Regardless of your grade level, your years as an educator, and the district in which you teach, the teacher-to-administrator relationship will affect your career for better or worse. A good relationship has a positive effect on the teacher—and on the students as well. Isn't that positive impact on students why we are all in the profession?

The meeting between Mrs. Towns and Ms. Walker had all the right feelings. But why? Based on the opening anecdote, we can conclude that their relationship is based on trust, professionalism, and, ultimately, a focus on the overall growth of the teacher.

An administrative team that supports you, contributes to your professional learning, and sees you first as a human being is one that will sustain you in the field of education. School administrations run the whole gamut from poor to excellent. If you have one that allows your voice to be heard and respects you as a professional, you are in a winning position.

The bottom line is that the teacher-to-administrator relationship can be an early indicator of the overall success of a school. It has been said that a school is typically a direct reflection of the administrative team leading it. To fully engage in the work of education, the teacher-to-administrator relationship must be built on a foundation of trust and authenticity. We must also remember that this relationship involves a power differential, which is important to acknowledge. However, trying to lessen the feelings behind the power differential will help to create a system that everyone can feel a part of. For that to happen, the first element in a positive relationship—trust—must be present.

Trust

Trust is something that is built over time in the smallest moments. The administration serves as the leadership of the school, and so demonstrating trust is crucial. Often it is that model from the top that flows into the other areas of the school building.

We know that trust is a major factor in any relationship, but trust on both sides is particularly vital in the teacher-to-administrator relationship. Teachers want to know that leadership is going to do what they say they are going to do; follow-through is essential. They want to know their voice matters, that they are all a part of the educational community, and that the collaborative vision set by all is being carried out. They also want to trust their leadership to keep the main thing—students—first, along with teacher well-being. On the other side, administrators also need to see trust embedded in the relationship. They need to trust that the educators who engage with students every day are doing what they say they are going to do, that children are being treated fairly and justly in the classrooms. They need to know that the school's collaborative vision is also being carried out by the education community they lead.

It's important to recognize that trust can be built in pockets of the school building, even if it doesn't start and flow from the top. The more people are reliable, follow through with what they say, own their wrongdoings, and show that they support the school's vision, the more trust is built. Imagine that everyone has a personal "trust jar," and each time someone builds an aspect of trust, a marble gets placed in the jar. Close your eyes. Can you visualize that? When someone breaks your trust, it's like a marble slowly rolling right out of the jar.

Remember that we discussed the "rooms of trust" in Chapter 1. Think about where your teacher-to-administrator relationship falls and which room you are in. You may not be in the break room (aka the "four-walls trust" room), and that is completely OK. However, we should be continually building and restoring relationships to be able to be in the front lobby of surface-level trust, and even, eventually, in the break room (see Figure 1.2 on p. 10).

One way to ensure the stabilization of trust is to know that everyone is being who they truly are—their authentic selves. As in other relationships, authenticity is an essential factor.

Authenticity

As we have noted before, being your authentic self means staying true to who you are, what your values are, and what you believe in. There is a lot of discussion about what it looks like to be your true authentic self in every space and how liberating it can be. However, what if the school in which you work doesn't accept the "authentic" you as the classroom educator or the administrator? How do you navigate that space? What does that feel like? On the flip side, what does it look and feel like when your school fully embraces the authentic you?

Being your full authentic self does not have to mean showing full vulnerability to everyone in your school environment. Although being vulnerable can help to build authentic and meaningful relationships, it must be done against a backdrop of trust that allows everyone to feel safe. Being your full authentic self should not require you to "keep it real" one hundred percent of the time. Everything has a time and place.

With that being said, there will be a few people within your school community who are allowed to see the full essence of your authentic self. Those are the people with whom you are completely vulnerable, the smaller community within your larger school environment, and folks that you have built trust with. The authentic self is who you are, how you identify, what you value, and what you believe. You must be able to be yourself at work, especially with those you interact with directly. If you are unable to do so, you will have to give some thought to the underlying "why" and determine if the cause is something within you or within your school environment. Otherwise, ignoring the situation can begin to have a negative effect on the relationship with your administrators or your staff, and it can also affect your mental health. Do that reflective work for yourself.

Ways to Build, Maintain, and Restore Teacher-to-Administrator Relationships

Building, maintaining, and restoring the teacher-to-administrator relationship can follow many paths. It may mean stepping out of your comfort zone and meeting with your administration with new ideas, suggestions, or questions. Sometimes just speaking up at meetings and being forthcoming helps your administrators get to know you, and vice versa. Doing so may mean taking a risk (for better or worse), but it can build a bridge—the relationship bridge. Sometimes it even means confronting a difficult or uneasy situation head on, in a respectful manner. It may mean digging into your emotions, especially those related to fear, anger, and sadness. Whatever the case may be, there are various ways to build, maintain, and even restore the teacher-to-administrator relationship. Let's examine some options.

Build

Building the teacher-to-administrator relationship means thinking of each other as humans first, as individuals with emotions and feelings. There are many ways to start the building phase. The following are some examples.

Share mutual respect. The Dalai Lama once stated, "Mutual respect is the foundation of genuine harmony" (Men-Tsee-Khang, 2015). When you have mutual respect, you value each other; you value each other's opinions. You make space and listen for ideas and innovation, and you collaborate on decisions that may or may not align with your own. You take the time to look at another person's perspective.

What does mutual respect look like for you? During times you felt respected, what has been done to foster that? How do you show others that you respect them? If you are having a hard time answering these questions, think about what would increase the likelihood of being respected or demonstrating respect to others—including your administrators or staff.

Mutual respect is a way to begin cultivating community. It is a cornerstone of really being able to build, maintain, and restore. In any relationship, mutual respect has to be front and center, a staple.

Align your vision. A vision is the ultimate goal, where we see ourselves in the future. It reflects the school's values and objectives. It is important for your workplace to have a vision that aligns with your values. For instance, if you believe that equity and belonging should be at the center of the work that you do and those elements are not a part of your school's vision, the result will be a continual conflict, either internal or external.

If you work in a space where the vision doesn't align with your values, whether you are a teacher or an administrator, it is time to do one of two things. The first is to use your voice to advocate for and try to influence a shared vision that is created collaboratively; this would be the time to set up a committee or involve the entire staff in the creation or revamping of the vision. The second is to bring about periodic reviews of the vision; ideally, this should happen at least three times a year. At the beginning of the year, ask yourselves, together, *Is this our vision and what we value?* Then in the middle of the year, collectively check in by asking, *Are we upholding our vision and our values?* Lastly, look at the vision at the end of the year to reflect and make necessary changes for the following year.

The vision statement should not be empty words. It should be created, followed, and revisited in an authentic way. If you find that the collective vision and values of the school do not align with what you value, you must ask yourself, *Is this a space where I want to continue to do my work? Is this the space where I can uphold what I value when educating children?* Those are difficult but essential questions to ask. At the end of the day, having a similar vision that is aligned to your values is crucial to your work, whether you are an administrator or a teacher—and whether you decide to stay or to leave.

Recognize communication as key. Communication is a huge piece in building a relationship, and it should take place both when things are going well and when things are a bit stressful. Let administrators know how you are feeling. One thing is certain: administrators cannot read minds. Share your thoughts. However, if you decide to communicate about something that isn't going well, also be prepared with some thoughtful solutions to the problem. That helps.

The communication piece goes both ways. For administrators, communication with the entire staff is one way to build relationships, but individual communication is also important. Let individual teachers know when they are doing things that you see as having a positive impact and why. It's one thing to shout-out folks in groups; it's a whole other thing to personalize the communication. The same goes when things are not so great. If something you want to communicate does not affect the entire staff—for instance, if a teacher is regularly coming in late, leaving students waiting at the classroom door—an email to the entire staff is unnecessary. Instead, a quick check-in with that person is all that is required, including finding out if there's something going on that's causing the problem and if they're OK. Remember to always begin with positive intent.

Get to know each other. You may be saying, "Of course it's important for teachers to get to know their administrators and for administrators to get to know their teachers." However, this "getting to know you" behavior is not always intentional throughout the school year. Common icebreakers at the beginning of the school year definitely help, but what happens after the school year has begun? One way to get to know each other better is to periodically and purposefully check in with each other. That means administrators checking in on teachers and teachers checking in with their administrators. Some teachers may feel challenged to fight against the inherent power differential, but remember, your administrator faces some of the same life challenges you do, and a check-in can go a long way—especially when you sense that someone is having a hard day. Doing so shows that people on both sides of the relationship care about each other, knowing that the job can get difficult at times. In addition to expanding the effort to get to know each other, checking in provides a way to extend support.

Follow through with expectations. Follow-through is important for both teachers and administrators. Doing what you say you are going to do is critical in building relationships. Once a person knows that you are going to do what is expected and maybe even exceed expectations, building a relationship becomes easier. When someone does not follow through and does not explain why (because we are all human, right?), the shortcoming begins to shake the metaphorical trust jar we referred to earlier. Following through helps to keep the marbles in the jar.

Try not to take things personally. An administrator once said that as a teacher, you have to worry about your classroom's four walls and the folks within those walls. However, the administration has to make sure the whole mothership and everyone in it is doing well. That observation may put teachers "in their place" a bit, but it does not mean that their voice is not valid or that what they are suggesting or saying does not matter to the administration. It means that many decisions are made from the viewpoint of a majority lens, by someone who can see more of the picture at play. For the individual teacher, it means trying not to react by taking things personally, which can be hard at times. Sometimes an administrative decision may feel very personal, but most of the time it isn't.

Be an active listener. Being an active listener means listening with your whole heart, not just your brain. Sounds strange, huh? Active listening is taking the time to really listen to what is being said and not try to read between the lines or make any judgments. We know that doing so can be challenging, but listening with positive intent to the person in front of you is important. And again, this approach applies both ways: teachers listening to administrators and administrators listening to teachers. Being an active listener helps to build bridges and allows space for honesty, communication, and trust to grow.

Be a learner. You may wonder how being a learner helps to build relationships, but consider this: anytime we can take a learner's stance, no matter the position we hold, we end up cultivating relationships because we realize we don't know all the answers. We have a lot to learn from each other, from our own experiences, and from our students. Vowing to always be a learner allows us to be open to possibility. Being a learner also means that we embody a growth mindset and allow for mistakes to be made in pursuit of learning.

Put boots on the ground as an expression of "servant leadership." Any time we see school leaders doing the work of the school alongside their staff, we are in awe. "Boots on the ground" is not a top-down leadership approach but rather a "We are in this thing together" approach. It is an approach that helps build relationships. It demonstrates that we are doing this work together—for each other and, above all, for the kids. This approach, which puts service to others at the core of the work, is what is often referred to as "servant leadership."

Maintain

Maintaining positive teacher-to-administrator relationships requires authenticity and intentionality in many areas, including communication in its various forms, striving to be compassionate when dealing with others, and keeping an optimistic outlook. Here are some ways to approach the maintenance phase of the teacher-to-administrator relationship.

Express your appreciation for each other. When it comes to communicating, one can never go wrong with expressing appreciation. Appreciation is a key factor in maintaining good relationships. Without it, one or the other party will likely begin to feel devalued.

Getting to know your colleagues' "work love language" can help you to appreciate them in a way that is meaningful to them. If you do not know what a work love language is, we suggest you explore the insights of Gary Chapman and Paul White (2019), authors of the audiobook *The 5 Languages of Appreciation in the Workplace*. Here are a couple examples of our personal favorites: receiving a nice sticky note complimenting you on something you were observed doing well in your classroom (words of affirmation); a colleague covering lunch and recess duty for you (acts of service).

Expressing and receiving appreciation is important for both teachers and administrators. Neither teaching nor leading is an easy job, and letting people know that you see and appreciate the work they are doing provides much-needed support and can sustain them through the difficult days. If expressing appreciation is not something that comes naturally to you, put a reminder note in your calendar to ensure that you don't overlook this aspect of communication. It makes a difference.

Recognize communication is a two-way street: teachers-to-administrators, administrators-to-teachers. Sometimes we communicate too much, but little or no communication is challenging in both the teacher and administrator realms. When an administrative decision is made that affects most or all of the people in the building and there is no communication about its purpose and how it should be executed, it will be hard to gain teacher support. Sometimes leaders have no control over administrative decisions, but it is still important to explain the purpose and the "why" as much as possible. Transparency cultivates trust and respect.

Teacher-to-administrator communication is just as important. Disagreement about a decision or a sense that the decision does not align with the school vision should be followed by a check-in with the administration. It is possible that the central office had a role in the decision, which perhaps was based on information you were unaware of. On the personal side, if something is happening in your life outside school that may affect your work, give your administration a heads-up. You do not have to disclose everything that is going on, but remember that administrators are not mind readers; they should have enough information to understand your circumstances.

Ask questions for clarification. Again, this point applies to both administrators and teachers. Lead from a place of curiosity and care. If you do not know, take the time to ask for clarification. Doing so actually saves time and avoids going around in "thinking circles" that develop around an untold number of assumptions and "what ifs." Just ask the question to the person directly involved. Don't allow yourself to waste time in thinking circles.

Be compassionate. Be a compassionate teacher. Be a compassionate leader. We all have things going on in our lives in and out of school. Let's not forget that. Let's not forget that we are all human beings and doing the best we can. Does that mean that there aren't areas where all of us can *do* better and *be* better? Absolutely not. However, let compassion be threaded through all the work that we do.

Find the good. It is often easier to find the negative, but what if we try to focus on the good instead? Wouldn't it feel better to notice what's good about our administrators? Our teachers? What if we started there? What would that look like? What would that feel like? There is almost always something good we can acknowledge, and starting at that point can provide an opportunity to dive into situations that may not be as good. Ultimately, this approach can lead to turning a not-so-good situation into one that is better—a step on the journey to becoming truly "good."

Restore

Restoration can be a challenging place to be in this relationship. In discussing how to approach this phase, let's name the "thing": sometimes schools have a "teachers versus administrators" undercurrent. We can feed into that undercurrent, or we can take steps to eliminate the "versus" component. Eliminating it may be challenging, but it is not impossible. For teachers, a bad relationship with an administrator can lead to early burnout, loss of passion for teaching, a change in school, a career change, and even health issues. For an administrator, a bad relationship with teachers can lead to a poor rate of staff retention, low morale, and lack of trust.

The COVID-19 pandemic offers a stark example. The pandemic multiplied the level of teacher stress (and administrator stress as well). In an article entitled "Teachers Are Not OK, Even Though We Need Them to Be," Madeline Will (2021) notes that in a survey conducted during the pandemic, 42 percent of teachers stated that "administrators [had] not made any efforts to help relieve their stress." We can easily speculate that this lack of attention had a negative effect on the teacher-to-administrator relationship. Furthermore, we may also posit that administrators were unable to relieve their own stress, which led to an inability to address the stress of their staff.

Even without the extraordinary conditions caused by the pandemic, educators in recent years have had to meet the demands of more mandates, more tests, more initiatives, more programs—in short, more *things* on their plates. All of these can create tension between administrators and teachers, causing the relationship to take a hit.

The good news is that both teachers and administrators can restore the relationship. It can happen through mutual respect, courage, listening, and humility. The restoration process requires both sides to be honest about their emotions, clear about what has happened or is happening, and willing to apologize if they were wrong. Both must also have an ear that is open, expansive, and receptive to the possibility of restoration. All of those things must be in place or in the process of being built in order to restore relationships between teachers and administrators. It is not an easy journey, but it can happen. Here are some ideas for getting off the ground.

Be honest about your feelings. Emotional awareness is important. Part of that awareness is being able to zero in on how you feel and to express those feelings in a safe space. If you have that safe space, be honest about what may be affecting you at work. The cause could be a decision that was made or something that someone said. However, no one can help until they know how you feel. Try to be as honest as possible about your feelings—but only if you feel safe enough to do so. In the event you don't feel safe, talk to someone who is within your trusted personal circle. This confidant may even be someone who is not in your school. Taking the necessary time to process is the first step, and verbally expressing your feelings is the next step. Sometimes the safe space we desire is outside our school building, and that's OK. However, those feelings may ultimately require verbalization in your school.

Initiate conversations about any issues concerning yourself and your classroom. Instead of dealing with everything on your own island, take a moment to schedule a meeting or have a conversation with the administrator about any issues you are having. Doing so helps to build a community in the school building, and it demonstrates the transparency that enables a continuing effort to restore the relationship.

Be OK with respectful confrontation. Figure 6.1 is a form that will help you to sort out your feelings and be able to think through the issue or issues you are having, as well as come up with some solutions. You can complete it before having a conversation with the other person or persons involved.

Prepare to restore what's broken, including being ready to acknowledge personal fault, if pertinent. Have an open mind and an open heart as you think about what may be causing a breakdown in the teacher-to-administrator relationship. Be ready to acknowledge any personal fault if that is a valid point. At the same time, be in a space that allows you to be able to accept the personal faults of others. Remember, we are all humans, and we will make mistakes.

FIGURE 6.1

Reflection Form for Respectful Confrontation

Let's Reflect	
What happened?	
Who did it involve?	
When did it happen?	
How did it make you feel?	
Why do you think it happened?	
What are some solutions within your control?	

* * *

Figure 6.2 highlights the main points related to building, maintaining, and restoring teacher-to-administrator and administrator-to-teacher relationships. You can use it as a guide and reminder of ways to ensure your efforts are on the right path.

FIGURE 6.2

Ways to Build, Maintain, and Restore Relationships Between Teachers and Administrators

Relationship Type	Build	Maintain	Restore
Teacher-to-Administrator	• Get to know your administrators. • Be authentically you (in a respectful way). • Communicate with your administrators. • Align your vision. • Check in on your administrators periodically. • Try not to take things personally. • Follow through on expectations. • Remain professional, but don't be a doormat. • Be open to suggestions. • Be an active listener. • Be a learner.	• Let your administrators know that you appreciate their leadership (via note, email, conversation, etc.). • Continue to communicate with administrators. • Ask questions for clarification. • Continue to follow through with expectations.	• Be honest about your feelings. • Initiate a conversation about any issues concerning yourself and your classroom. • Be OK with respectful confrontation, using the form in Figure 6.1.
Administrator-to-Teacher	• Get to know your teachers. • Check in on your teachers' well-being. • Be genuinely invested. • Communicate your vision and expectations. • Actively support your teachers.	• Do ongoing check-ins. • Be compassionate. • Find the good. • Model and promote professional growth. • Continue to praise in simple but authentic ways.	• Identify the issue(s) that need to be resolved. • Remember the power differential. • Prepare to restore what's broken; be ready to acknowledge personal fault, if pertinent.

(continued)

FIGURE 6.2—*(continued)*

Ways to Build, Maintain, and Restore Relationships Between Teachers and Administrators

Relationship Type	Build	Maintain	Restore
Administrator-to-Teacher	• Praise your teachers both collectively and individually. • Implement coaching conversations with teachers to help them grow. • Model learning and growing. • Follow through. • Have your boots on the ground (servant leadership). • Be flexible. • Be an active listener. • Be a learner. • Remain professional. • Build authentically. • Delegate certain tasks to colleagues, which may relieve some task-related stress.	• Continue to have your boots on the ground, in the trenches (servant leadership). • Communicate—overly communicate. • Continue to communicate your vision and expectations. • Be flexible.	• Confront the challenge; have the difficult conversation. • Assume positive intent. • Continue to build, maintain, and restore.

Observations from Michael and Nita

Michael's Observations

Whenever I think about my first year in the school system, I think about my principal and the relationship I had with her. As a male counselor, I was often asked about my role in the building and whether or not I was frequently called upon for disciplinary issues or viewed as a mentor for all the male students. The short answer is "Yes!" I was involved in many decisions related to disciplinary issues, and I was viewed as a mentor for many students. My principal was not only comfortable and confident in who she was but could see that I was the same. She viewed me as an asset and allowed me to excel at my strengths while offering additional support to improve my weaknesses.

She was my first principal, my introduction to educational leadership. I must say, I couldn't have asked for a better school leader. She was phenomenal! Notice all of the past tense verbiage? I said "was" a lot of times, right? During my fourth year in education, my highly regarded principal was transferred to another school. I remember something I used to say before entering the education profession: "Education is a lot like politics." I learned how true that statement was. After years of growing little learners and building a thriving community, my principal was rewarded by being moved to a new school and challenged to replicate her past success. After she left, I had a difficult time adjusting to the new principal.

Adjustment to change is challenging. Trying to navigate new expectations and form new working relationships requires effort. Even though I was aware of the upcoming change in administration, I had a difficult time. Not wanting your principal to leave and having to adapt to a new one is not among those feel-good topics that educators talk about, but there are relational aspects that can make the transition easier. As the time approached, I collected my thoughts, but I still couldn't prepare myself for the shift in school culture headed my way. I was angry, resentful, and even somewhat resistant to change. Even as I take this trip down memory lane, I still believe my feelings were valid and justifiable. Furthermore, if the same circumstances occurred again, my sentiments would be nearly identical.

Without going into detail, I can state that I drew from previous experience and knowledge, as well as determination and support to eventually get through that difficult time. Resilience often shows up when you have these things backing you up. My support came in the form of my wife and my colleagues. All were instrumental in helping me process and work through the tumultuous experience. Sometimes we forget the profound importance of those relationships. They can and will carry us through some of the most challenging moments of our careers. In my particular situation, I learned something—something I knew but had forgotten: the power and strength of our support system can keep us sane or drive us to the breaking point. I'm so thankful for my support system.

Nita's Observations

After working in the field of education for 18 years, I have had my share of principals. Ten, to be exact. Of course, each had a different personality type. The consistent factor in working in different buildings and with different leaders was me. However, I had to constantly reflect on what I needed in order to feel valued, respected, and supported in each space and under a variety of leadership styles. The more experience I gained in education, the more I was able to know what I needed, what my students needed, and what the collective staff needed in my workspace.

The challenge is, the needs change; you change. You have to start with getting to know yourself. How do you know what you need if you don't dig into that work of knowing yourself and what you need to be a good teacher? One way that I dug into that self-work was checking in on my feelings. If I was upset about something my administrator did or said, I would ask myself to think about what made me upset and why. Then I would ask myself if I could confront that situation head-on—in a respectful way.

I will be honest. There were some administrators I felt I could confront and engage in open discussions, and others that made me feel it wasn't safe to do so. In those latter situations, I asked myself why I didn't feel that I could have a voice and that my voice would be respected. I would ask if that space was one that I could influence or change, or if it was a space that I needed to release myself from. I was able to change some spaces, but I had to release myself from others. But I never left without doing the work within myself first.

The teacher-to-administrator relationship is really important to the culture of the school. Everyone must do their part to "BMR" that relationship. It is not easy, but never impossible. In my case, I had to remember a point that we have mentioned several times: that we are all humans first, and we are never perfect.

Reflective Questions

- Think about the word *trust*. How do you think your teacher-to-administrator relationship fares when it comes to trust?
- Has there been a time when you felt like you had a strong relationship with your administrators or teachers? What did that look, sound, and feel like?
- As a teacher or an administrator, which factor is most important in establishing a relationship with your colleague: mutual respect, authenticity, trust, or aligned/similar vision?
- Why do you think that is the case?
- How is your relationship with your administrators or teachers? What are some things that could happen to strengthen the relationship? What are some things you can continue doing?

7 Teacher-to-Staff Relationships

Ms. Johnson has been teaching for seven years. This year she has been working with Mr. Samuels, a paraprofessional, in her classroom. She has found Mr. Samuels to be most helpful. Any time she asks him to make copies or do lunchroom and hallway duty for her, he does it. Having an extra set of hands has been so useful.

On this particular Tuesday, Ms. Johnson could tell that Mr. Samuels was not getting things done as efficiently as he normally did. When she asked him to make copies, he snapped at her, stating that he was not her little errand boy. He then stormed out of the room, leaving Ms. Johnson holding the stack of papers and wondering what she had done wrong. She also wondered, what was wrong with Mr. Samuels?

In between classes, Mr. Samuels still hadn't returned, and Ms. Johnson began chatting with Mrs. Stein, the teacher in the neighboring classroom, about what had happened. As she was telling her the story, Mr. Samuels walked through the door shaking his head and waving his hand. Ms. Johnson knew she needed to talk to him before the next class began. She rarely does well in such conversations; they make her uncomfortable. However, the conversation had to happen, because they work together every day.

Why Teacher-to-Staff Relationships Are Important

When most people think about education, they typically think about the teachers, the students, and the administrative team. Each is important, but who is missing from that list? Administrative assistants, bookkeepers, custodians, counselors, food service workers, librarians, occupational therapists, instructional coaches, school psychologists, speech pathologists, social workers, and technology support technicians are all high-priority stakeholders. Every day, school staff significantly assist in ensuring that students remain the primary focus of education. Teachers are often thrust into difficult situations that require the assistance of support staff. Whether it's dealing with disruptive student behavior, locating resources, determining student achievement levels, or identifying disabilities, support staff are often the glue that keeps schools together throughout the school year.

Studies have shown that teacher-to-staff relationships can significantly affect teachers' relationships with students, teacher retention, and overall school culture (Barth, 2006). Take a moment to think about a staff member in your school building with whom you have a solid working relationship. Now think about a staff member with whom you might not have a good working relationship. How does each of these relationships affect your work as a classroom teacher?

When educators' relationships with support staff are not strong, everyone suffers. Consider the vignette that introduced this chapter. Mr. Samuels stormed out of the classroom when Ms. Johnson asked him to make copies—something she had requested many times before. We can speculate about the reason behind Mr. Samuels's reaction. He might have felt underappreciated or treated as "less than"; but we will never know the actual cause until he and Ms. Johnson have a conversation.

Everyone—support staff included—wants appreciation and to feel like their job is purposeful. These feelings arise from strong teacher-to-staff relationships, and, once again, trust and authenticity are foundational factors.

Trust

In positive school environments, educators typically develop a working synergy with colleagues. They collaborate on many things, such as creating lesson plans; they watch over one another's students; and they advocate for one another. Such environments don't necessarily start out that way but are built over time, based on trust.

Much like all of the other relationships in a school building, teacher-to-staff relationships cannot blossom without trust. At a minimum, teachers must trust that support staff people will do exactly what they are tasked with doing. Communicating expectations, knowing what everyone's "job" is, and *valuing* everyone's job builds trust and cultivates a culture of respect.

Authenticity

We have discussed authenticity in the other chapters in this book, and we know you now understand how important and fulfilling it is to "be yourself" in relationships. The teacher-to-staff relationship is no different. Continue to be authentic, and encourage support staff members to do the same. When communication is open and everyone in the educational space feels safe and valued, authenticity is usually easy to achieve.

Ways to Build, Maintain, and Restore Teacher-to-Staff Relationships

Building, maintaining, and restoring teacher-to-staff relationships is essential in creating a welcoming and thriving school community. Support staff are the people who provide much needed assistance so that your primary focus can be on the students in your classroom. In many cases, they can have an enormous impact on your success.

Let's think again about Ms. Johnson in the introductory vignette. She didn't realize that she had probably been asking Mr. Samuels to do more tasks than he could reasonably handle, pushing him to the point of exhaustion and frustration. She may have missed nonverbal warning signs from him. However, his inability or unwillingness to advocate for himself put both parties in a tough position due to lack of communication.

A harmonious relationship between educators and staff can significantly enhance everyone's morale because it contributes to a pleasant work environment. Of course, the same is true of other relationships, but the teacher-to-staff relationship is uniquely situated to assist educators and students. Many staff people work side-by-side with teachers and students or provide the essential behind-the-scenes services, such as small groups and 1:1 support, that contribute to success in the classroom.

Build

As with other relationships, the building phase of teacher-to-staff relationships starts with open communication. It is also important to keep in mind that kindness matters. Work from the mindset of treating others the way you wish to be treated. The following are a few specific suggestions for building strong teacher-to-staff relationships.

Welcome staff into your environment. Educators are often consumed by concerns over what is happening within the four walls of the classroom, but taking the time to welcome support staff into your domain extends a sense of community. This simple gesture makes everyone feel like they are an active part of your classroom—which they are. When you need assistance with a disruptive student, you usually call a counselor. When you need assistance handling a spill or a bathroom accident, you contact a custodian. When one of your students can't remember her cafeteria PIN number, you likely contact a food service worker.

Being welcoming makes it more likely that people will be more willing not only to help you, but also to establish an amicable relationship. Welcoming can take many forms. For instance, if you have a teacher's assistant, make sure that person has a space in your room to call her own. This could be something as simple as a table or a desk that makes the staff member feel like part of the classroom community—and it allows students to see the person in that way as well.

Speak to *everyone* you encounter. We know this gesture sounds simple and maybe even ridiculous or pointless, but a verbal greeting establishes an instant connection between people (Gentile et al., 2019). We often hear about students who feel "unseen," partly because no one acknowledges them. Staff may feel the same way. When we greet others, we can help to set the tone for their day and ours. Just remember to not take it personally if someone does not greet you in return. As we have noted many times, we are all human, and sometimes our minds are distracted by thoughts of the many things we have to do.

Get to know and value everyone's role and keep expectations reasonable. Educators sometimes develop tunnel vision. They're only able to see what lies before them in their particular purview. Once they enter the tunnel, the role and contribution of school staff may be minimized or devalued. Although this mindset may not be intentional, it still happens and has a lasting impact on the relationship. When teachers become stressed and feel pressure related to such things as the need to meet deadlines, show student growth, and actively participate in meetings or trainings, they are more likely to minimize everyone else's role. They may also make unreasonable demands of support staff, such as asking for 500 copies of an agenda on the morning of an event that was planned weeks before. Such situations can strain teacher-to-staff relationships. Of course, emergency situations may happen, but when unreasonable demands occur regularly, grace is less likely extended. Remember that everyone's role contributes to the school's functioning and effectiveness, and everyone's role holds value. Take time to appreciate the "little" things that staff members do for you and for the overall school community.

Communicate your needs. As we have said before, no one is a mind reader—not even the most qualified and educated professionals in the building. This reality means that we must communicate our needs before we can expect them to be met. Often we know what we need or want to happen but, for whatever reason, fail to ask support staff who could help. We may complain about someone having no idea of what should be done without stopping to consider that it is unrealistic to expect a need to be met if we haven't communicated it. Take the time to communicate. Doing so will make your days run much more smoothly.

Create a "favorite things" list. We all love gifts of appreciation, and giving and receiving unexpected gifts can be a way to build relationships and boost morale. One way to make sure the recipient will actually appreciate the birthday or holiday gift is to have everyone in the building fill out a form like the one shown in Figure 7.1.

FIGURE 7.1

Favorite Things List

Name:
Birthday:
Favorite place to shop:
Favorite place to eat:
Favorite place to get coffee:
Favorite gift card:
Favorite candy:
Favorite snack:
Favorite color:
Favorite thing to do for self-care:

Maintain

Maintaining positive teacher-to-staff relationships doesn't have to involve a detailed "grand plan." Simple communications may be all that is necessary. Remember, some relationships will be easier to maintain than others, but all are worth the effort. What follows are some suggestions for how to maintain good teacher-to-staff relationships.

Check in periodically, even if the exchange is brief. It's easy to check in with someone you see frequently, such as a teaching assistant, but make an effort to reach out to those you see only occasionally as well. Check-ins can be as simple as asking how someone's weekend went or reminding them to take some time for themselves. The nature and duration of the check-in will vary, depending on how close your relationship is.

Meet a minimum of two to three times a year to align on goals for students. This helps when the staff working with you come in to provide support in the classroom. It allows the relationship with each other and the students to remain the focus. It also helps with student success in the classroom community.

Restore

As with other relationships, the teacher-to-staff relationship can break down for a variety of reasons. Restoration can be difficult, but it's important to not let a negative feeling persist over time. Here are a few suggestions for when and if the relationship needs to be restored.

Offer a sincere apology when necessary. One of the best ways to restore any relationship is to offer a sincere apology if you have done something that has had a negative impact. So many things happen in the midst of a typical school day, and some people develop the tunnel vision we mentioned earlier—seeing only the tasks ahead of them or their individual concerns. The result can be inadvertent slights and dismissals of feelings. Such occurrences are avoidable, but they happen. For example, you may be heading back to your classroom to prep your students for a district assessment; you're in that tunnel, and you don't hear the administrative assistant greeting you and telling you to check your mailbox. Because you don't return the greeting or check your mailbox, the administrative assistant thinks you're rude and dismissive. A sincere apology can alleviate the misunderstanding and get your relationship back on track.

Allow space and time for restoration to occur. In the midst of a disagreement or misunderstanding, you may not be able to reach an amicable resolution. Taking space and time to step away from the situation can lead to greater perspective by both parties and acknowledgment of personal faults. In short, it's easier to see the full picture when you step away from it briefly.

Be willing to compromise. Remember, a compromise is an amicable solution for all parties involved. Sacrifice is a necessary component of a successful compromise, and all parties have to be willing to come to the table and sacrifice something they wanted for someone else's gain. However, everyone typically gains in the end. Regardless of the circumstances, a compromise may not only resolve a specific situation but also serve as a fundamental step in restoring relationships overall.

* * *

Figure 7.2 highlights the main points related to building, maintaining, and restoring teacher-to-staff relationships. You can use it as a guide and reminder of ways to ensure your efforts are on the right path.

FIGURE 7.2

Ways to Build, Maintain, and Restore Teacher-to-Staff Relationships

Build	Maintain	Restore
• Welcome people into your environment. • Greet everyone. • Value everyone's role in the building. • Communicate your needs. • Offer tokens of appreciation.	• Express appreciation. • Continue to communicate needs. • Check in to see how people are doing, including what's going on in their lives outside school.	• Offer a sincere apology when necessary. • Allow space and time for restoration to take place. • Be willing to compromise. • Understand how unresolved issues can be detrimental to a positive relationship.

SPEAKING FROM EXPERIENCE:
Observations from Michael and Nita

Michael's Observations

It's human nature to wonder what someone else is doing in your building. What I mean is, when you're a classroom teacher and you're in the throes of a school year, you want to know the *who*, *what*, *when*, *where*, and *how*. Specifically, *who* is going to help me, *what* are they going to do, *when* are they going to do it, *where* is it going to happen, and *how* can they help me.

I found this out quickly, toward the end of my first year in education. I remember feeling like my first year as the school counselor had been a relative success. As I saw it, students and staff were familiar with me and were aware of my responsibilities in the building. We were headed down the home stretch of the school year, those last four or five weeks when teachers were stressed and overwhelmed with testing. As tensions throughout the building rose, we were informed of an impending change in school administration. Shortly after the new administrator arrived, she interviewed classroom teachers, by grade level, to determine immediate needs. Teachers took the opportunity to air personal grievances and spread misinformation about support staff. During one meeting, teachers stated they didn't know what the counselor did in the building and had never seen any lessons discussing social-emotional learning.

With one simple conversation, an entire grade level's relationship with the school counselor—me—could be significantly damaged. Although I had believed classroom teachers understood my role in the building, I was mistaken. Even though I had believed it was common knowledge that a school counselor's role is to address the social and emotional needs of students, I was mistaken. Either I had not been intentional enough or the stress of high-stakes testing, administrative change, and overall dissatisfaction with the current state of education was to blame. Somehow the entire school year went by, and there I was, thinking teachers understood my role, thinking I had developed a solid working relationship with teachers. I learned otherwise.

That experience was pivotal, and it reaffirmed my belief that you can do all that you can, but some will be displeased. Fortunately, I didn't allow myself to get jaded, and I focused even more on the students and families I was serving. As a result, I didn't have time to ponder or become frustrated over the opinions of others. This approach was crucial to my maintaining a positive attitude even though others around me weren't so positive.

Nita's Observations

I believe that everyone in the school building matters, that everyone helps the school operate. Everyone is inherently a "teacher," part of an environment where students and various adults connect with each other every day.

With that being the case, everyone holds a responsibility in the building and deserves to be respected and valued. In my experience, the best relationships are those characterized by mutual respect. I don't believe in a tiered system when it comes to humanity and treating others well. I remember being a 1st grade teacher and having a teacher's assistant come to help in my classroom. One thing I asked her was what she needed to be successful in her position. I usually offered a desk and space in the classroom community, but she did not want that. She said she just needed to know what I expected of her when she came into the classroom to assist students.

We decided to have an after-school meeting to discuss expectations. This meeting was a great time to get to know one another, find out what we valued, and determine how both of us, as educators in the same space, wanted the classroom community to run.

One thing that continued throughout our relationship was constant communication, which was essential, especially when a situation was confusing or schedules changed at the last minute. To be on the same page, we had to take the time to meet, discuss, and have open communication.

At the end of the year, this wonderful person said that our classroom was a place she loved to come to each day because she felt valued and respected. Her statement made me feel good, but it also made me wonder how things were in other spaces and how they could be made better for her and other staff members.

Reflective Questions

- What are some ways that you communicate with staff in the onset of the relationship?
- How do you welcome support staff into your classroom?
- What are some ways that staff members are appreciated in your classroom or school building?
- What can you do to be more intentional about making support staff feel valued and respected?

8 Virtual Relationships

Mrs. Brunswell was tasked to be the virtual teacher this year for students who chose the virtual-school option. She wasn't happy about taking on the role, but she was the most proficient teacher when it came to technology and could manage the various programs with ease. She organized a plan, put together a schedule, and emailed families about the times for virtual classes and work that had to be completed, along with due dates. Mrs. Brunswell had done all the things necessary to help her virtual teaching run smoothly.

However, as time went on, she mentioned to some of her fellow teachers that she didn't feel connected to her students. She noticed that some of the students had "fallen off" and were not attending her live teaching sessions. They weren't turning in work and said they just didn't care.

Mrs. Brunswell began to feel she wasn't making a difference and her job didn't matter. She didn't want to continue being a virtual teacher and continuously complained about her job, her students, and their families. When she was offered professional learning, she refused to go, stating that being skilled in using technology was not the problem. It was the kids' lack of motivation. They were "done," and so was she.

Learning Through Virtual Teaching

Clearly, Mrs. Brunswell was not prepared to be a yearlong virtual teacher. She was a veteran educator who was proficient in technology but preferred teaching face-to-face. Not wanting to teach virtually made her resistant to learning new virtual-teaching strategies. She didn't want to create a connection with her students for fear that if she were too good, she would be stuck in the role of virtual teacher.

Like Mrs. Brunswell, many educators—despite years of experience, coursework, and professional development—were totally unprepared for the upheaval caused by the conversion to virtual learning during the COVID-19 pandemic. A global crisis upended education as we knew it. We wondered, how do we make those connections, extend the special handshakes, turn improvised lessons into deep conversations that students remember years from now? How in the world do those things happen, virtually?

You've probably heard the phrase "When you stop learning, you stop growing." Well, it's true. Learning is the essence of the work that we do as educators; we aren't exempt. It's just that usually we have time to engage in the learning, to practice, to try it out. But in the throes of the pandemic, our learning had to occur on the job. It had to be right now. We didn't have a choice and we weren't asked; as educators we just had to execute. We built the proverbial plane in midflight, even though most of us weren't ready. We did it. Some of us loved teaching virtually, and some of us did not. Either way, we were required to do it.

One thing we knew in the midst of the virtual teaching/virtual learning experience was that we had to build and maintain relationships with our students. The foundation of teaching, that relationship piece, was something we had before the pandemic and must continue to have now—even virtually.

But how can we do that if we can't see the students in person? How can we do that if a student's screen isn't turned on? How can we do that if students don't engage in the learning? How can we do that if students lack access to the necessary technology? How is building relationships even possible under such circumstances? In this chapter, we tackle these questions and provide some answers.

Equity and Access in the Virtual Space

Before we can discuss virtual teaching, we need to discuss the issue of ensuring that students, teachers, and staff have what they need in order to fulfill the expectations that have been presented to them. For instance, how can students take part in a live virtual teaching session without access to a technological device? If they have a device, how can they log on without adequate Wi-Fi access? Any discussion of virtual teaching has to address these questions related to equity and access.

During the pandemic, many students and their families had to drive or walk to schools and sit outside in order to access the schools' Wi-Fi. Some families didn't have enough devices for their children to use. This situation was unacceptable at the time, and it's unacceptable today. It is not OK to continue to move on with virtual instruction when students and even some teachers lack what they need to learn or to teach.

First things first: we must find out what our students have access to before we begin virtual teaching and learning. The best way to come up with answers is through the school administration or district office. For example, one approach could be to add an "Access to Technology" component to information forms that are collected from students and families at the beginning of the school year. Asking questions about access is a critical step that is often overlooked, to the detriment of teaching and learning. We have to make sure that students—and staff—have what they need to get the job done. Doing so is the essential starting point for making virtual connections.

In the next sections of this chapter, we provide some suggestions for building virtual versions of the various relationships we have discussed in the preceding chapters. We provide tips for maintaining those online connections as well.

Ways to Build and Maintain Virtual Relationships

Poor Mrs. Brunswell. She struggled with making initial connections with students, partly because she was reluctant to accept the position of virtual teacher in the first place and partly because she did not want to do anything extra to cultivate a new kind of relationship with her students. As a result, she suffered—and so did they.

As we have previously stated, the work of building and maintaining relationships is essential to successful teaching and learning. The virtual environment creates unique circumstances, but the foundational nature of the work is the same across all of the various relationships educators encounter.

Tips for Building and Maintaining Virtual Teacher-to-Student Relationships

Teacher-to-student relationships are at the heart of the virtual classroom. Here are some suggestions for how to build and maintain this key connection.

Conduct virtual student interviews throughout the year. Many teachers conduct student interviews at the beginning of the year, as a way to get to know their students' interests, likes and dislikes, and anything else that may be pertinent. We suggest continuing the conversation by meeting virtually at least two more times during the year.

For your initial conversations, set up a schedule of interviews lasting about 10 minutes each. You can hold these interviews before school begins or during the first few weeks of school. Either way, reach out to every single student by calling, sending an email, or using another approach that provides the link to the conversation. As you begin the interviews, ask students to turn on their screen so that you can see their face. Ideally, they will leave the screen on throughout the entire conversation so that you can better connect. However, be mindful that some students may not feel comfortable sharing their home space onscreen for various reasons, such as a reluctance to display living conditions; or they simply may not be ready to make themselves visible. Give them that choice and respect their preference. We suggest you keep notes of your interviews with each student so that when you have your next one-on-one conversation, you can remember the answers to some of the questions from your previous encounter.

Below are some interview questions for the beginning, middle, and end of the year. Of course, these are not the only questions you can ask, and some are questions you can ask whether you are in a virtual or a face-to-face conversation. Whatever the environment—virtual, face-to-face, or some mixture of the two—these questions will help to build and maintain a positive relationship with your students.

Sample Student Interview Questions for the Beginning of the Year

1. Do you have a nickname or a name you want to be called? (If the student has a nickname, ask how it came to be.)
2. What is the one thing you like most about yourself? What made you choose that?
3. What is one area in which you feel you need to grow or get better?
4. Tell me about your culture. How do you identify?
5. How do you feel about school? Why?
6. What is the best memory or story you can share about school?
7. Do you like learning virtually? Why or why not?
8. Do you like to keep your camera on or off while learning virtually?
9. Who is your favorite teacher? What makes or has made that teacher your favorite?
10. What is your favorite subject? Why?
11. What is your favorite book? What makes that book your favorite?
12. What is your favorite thing to do outside of school?
13. How can I support you in the virtual classroom? What makes you feel like a teacher is helping you?
14. What do you think is the best way you learn? Do you like to watch learning in action (e.g., modeling, demonstrations)? Do you like to learn with your hands? Do you like to read and take notes to learn?
15. What is a goal for yourself that can make this year even better than last year?

Sample Student Interview Questions for the Middle of the Year

1. How are things going for you?
2. What are some things you like about learning virtually in my class?
3. What are some things you don't like about learning virtually in my class?
4. How do you think you are doing in my class?
5. What has been amazing for you so far?
6. What has been challenging for you?
7. I've noticed that you don't like to keep your camera on during class. Is there a reason for that? (Reiterate that keeping the camera on helps you both to connect during class.)
8. What do you think you or I can do to make the rest of your year successful?
9. How do you think you are doing in attaining the goal you set of _____?
10. Let's revamp or set another goal. Are you OK with that?

Sample Student Interview Questions for the End of the Year

1. How has this year been for you?
2. What is one thing that you think has helped you this year?
3. What was your proudest moment from this year?
4. What was a challenge this year?
5. How do you think you did overall?
6. What is one thing you will take into next year to help you as a virtual learner?
7. How do you feel you did with the goal of _____? Did you master your goal?

These interview questions are meant to provide a guide for talking with your students individually. As you continue to build relationships, it will be easier to ask questions that connect directly to a particular student. Although it may be tempting to think you don't have time for one-on-one interviews, keep in mind their importance in building and maintaining positive, authentic relationships.

Allow students to have a voice in the virtual classroom.
Robert Marzano (n.d.) states that "engaging student voice in classroom discussions deepens content knowledge and supports higher
student achievement through constructing understanding and student engagement in learning." Although Marzano was referring to
in-person classroom situations, his observation applies to the virtual
classroom as well. When you allow students to use their voices, it also
begins to cultivate a relationship and sense of safety in your virtual
classroom community. Some ways to lift student voice and build community among the students would be using the chat box. Students can
also have time in the virtual lesson to unmute and share. Before doing
this, it is important to take some time to establish community agree-
ments so that students know routines, procedures, and what is acceptable within the virtual learning community.

**Use virtual platforms that maximize opportunities for stu-
dent engagement.** Choose from the variety of interactive platforms
that provide maximum engagement for students. These platforms
give students the opportunity to engage with one another more, share
their thoughts within the platform, watch interactive videos, play
learning games, and so on. If you are new to the virtual world or struggle with the use of virtual platforms, don't allow frustration to prevent
you from learning and growing in your knowledge. Ask for help. For
veteran teachers, that may mean asking younger colleagues for assistance or suggesting a professional learning session. If you don't ask for
help, no one may know you are struggling. Don't forget that your goal
is to engage with your students, to build connections with them. That
may require learning new things so that they, in turn, can learn.

Step into the world of social media. Become knowledgeable
about how to incorporate social media in your classroom. You don't
need to be an expert, but it helps to have some familiarity with the
major social media applications. Social media is often the way in
which most students become aware of current events. A mere mention
of one of these apps may spark an entire conversation. If you feel you
have become savvy enough to use these applications, try creating a
fun video to entertain your students. Another example of using social
media in the classroom would be using a video from a social media

influencer that is discussing history or a historical moment. Take that time to have your student learn how to research the truth in what they heard on that particular video from social media. They may find the video they heard is true or they may find that it is not, but you are teaching invaluable skills of questioning what they see and hear on social media and you have made a connection with your students as well. You'll be amazed at the "deposit" you will have made in your teacher-to-student relationship account.

Try the 2 × 10 method, virtually, with at-risk students. The 2 × 10 method is described in depth by Allen N. Mendler (2001) in his book *Connecting with Students*. The strategy is simple: spend 2 minutes per day for 10 days in a row talking with an at-risk student about anything he or she wants to talk about. How does that translate, virtually? For starters you have to get them to log on, which may mean using a virtual platform such as Nearpod or Pear Deck to spark student engagement because they are allowed to do more than just listen. The spark of student engagement is the entry point you may need to build and maintain a relationship with at-risk students.

Re-engage the disengaged. When you realize one of your students has become disengaged during a virtual lesson, take time to have an "In It to Win It" conversation with that individual. Send a private message via the virtual platform to encourage the student to re-engage. Be sure to set aside time to follow up with the student after the lesson to check in again. Check-ins are important for maintaining positive relationships with students who need an extra push to motivate them.

Tips for Building and Maintaining Virtual Teacher-to-Family Relationships

The discussion in Chapter 4 emphasized the importance of building positive teacher-to-family relationships. We want families to be our partners in educating the students we teach. Working together can help to ensure their student is successful, but cultivating that connection virtually can be challenging. It is not impossible, however. Here are some tips for building the virtual bridge from school to home.

Keep accurate contact information. Making sure you have accurate contact information for reaching parents is essential whether you are working in a virtual or a face-to-face environment.

Communicate positively. As stated in Chapter 4, contacting families to share students' positive behaviors or actions lays the foundation for a solid relationship. The Positive Intervention Plan, or PIP, can be shared virtually at the beginning, middle, and end of the year. Whatever method is used, it is essential to reach out to families regularly and keep them connected to their student's day-to-day learning. Sharing positive moments is a way to celebrate with families as well as the student.

Don't let troublesome issues fester. Parents want to know what is going on with their children. For instance, if a student has missed a couple of virtual classroom sessions, reach out to the family to gain insight as to the possible reason. Remember, you are doing so out of concern. Assuming you have built a solid foundation in your teacher-to-family relationship, it should be much easier to communicate about the not-so-bright spots in their child's virtual school experience.

Conduct virtual conferences. The pandemic made it necessary to conduct conferences with parents/families virtually. This is one practice that we believe should continue, even if schools are back to in-person teaching and learning. Virtual conferences allow families to stay informed about their student's progress when otherwise they might have to take time off from work or not be able to attend at all. Talking virtually builds the teacher-to-family bridge and provides space for consistent communication.

Let parents into the virtual classroom. Allow parents to be a part of the virtual learning environment. At the elementary level, let them read a book aloud. At any level, host a Career Day or Career Week during which parents describe their jobs. Let parents come into the virtual classroom to share their knowledge about content the students are learning.

Tips for Administrators in Building and Maintaining Virtual Relationships

As the old saying goes, "It's lonely at the top." The "top" is where the decisions are made, and your staff may not like or agree with some of those decisions. However, leadership has to happen and decisions have to be made, even in a virtual space, and that lonely feeling can be exacerbated under such circumstances. You may feel like you are not as connected to your staff, but that doesn't have to be the case. You can build relationships with your staff and other colleagues even virtually. Building relationships will make your job more enjoyable and lessen that feeling that you are living on a virtual island by yourself.

Hold virtual staff meetings. Your teachers and staff may roll their eyes at this one; however, holding 30- to 40-minute staff meetings virtually brings everyone together. Try to make the session fun. Begin with an ice breaker. Remember to ask how everyone is doing, and listen—really listen. Create a safe space with your staff to continue to cultivate a community with care at the center.

Check in with your teachers and staff. Just as you expect teachers to check in with students, do the same for your teachers and staff. Ask how you can support them, if there is anything they need, or if they just need to talk. Checking in with teachers and staff members individually helps to keep you informed and aware, and can relieve any anxiety or stress they may have.

Connect with other leaders. Take care of yourself. Let's repeat that: Take care of yourself. It helps to connect with other leaders who are in the trenches with you, the leaders who understand. Tap into virtual groups, other leaders in your district, or even others that you may have worked with before in different places. Doing so will help you remember that you aren't alone.

Tips for Building and Maintaining Virtual Teacher-to-Teacher and Teacher-to-Staff Relationships

Even in the virtual space, relationships are everything. It may feel harder and more challenging to be able to have connections and build relationships, but it is not impossible. Your intentionality must be that much greater. The focus on taking time to check in with colleagues, having a moment to say hello for a few minutes, sending a quick video, or even having coffee over Zoom can help you create an initial connection. The face-to-face connection will be essential here, especially when most of the contact in the virtual world is through written communication. It will be important to build and maintain these relationships virtually.

Use proper email/text messaging etiquette. In the virtual world, we often rely on communication through emails and chats via text messaging. Sometimes we are unable to determine sarcasm, jokes, or tone in the communication we receive—and, just as important, we may not realize how our messages will be interpreted at the other end. That email sent in haste or in irritation—could it have waited until we calmed down a bit and thought through our feelings? When considering the right or wrong way to compose an email or a text message, follow these guidelines:

- Eliminate the use of all caps unless you want to appear aggressive or seem like you are yelling.
- Try not to overuse exclamation marks or question marks. Using too many exclamation marks can seem like you are shouting. Sometimes using multiple question marks can suggest sarcasm. Remember that when a person gets an email or a text message from you, they try to figure out your "tone." Too many exclamation marks or question marks can lead to misinterpreting your intent.
- *Do not* "reply all" unless it is absolutely necessary. How do you feel when you are on the receiving end of an unnecessary "reply all"? Are you aggravated with the sender? It can be annoying to be copied on every email or to see every response in an email chain if the message is not relevant to you. As a sender, take time to check that you are communicating only with those who need to know the information, not with an entire grade level, staff, or administrative team, unless appropriate.

Hold virtual team meetings. Make sure you and your team are still meeting, even if you can't get together in person. Before the start of team meetings, take time to collaborate on building team norms (e.g., reviewing the agenda ahead of time, completing the items needed to have a successful meeting, having equity of voice) for the virtual space. Doing so will help keep things flowing smoothly during your meetings.

Virtual meetings can be a way to collaborate, to plan, to discuss upcoming virtual events, and even to get things off your chest. Your team will be your virtual accountability partners. Meeting virtually reminds you that you are "in this together." If you don't have a team to work with, find other colleagues in the virtual world. You may be surprised to find out how many teachers are teaching virtually. Make an effort to build community with them.

Be open to virtual hangouts. In the virtual world, everything is done through your computer or phone, whether it's team building or just chatting it up with teacher friends and colleagues. Instead of setting up time only for work-related issues such as team meetings, IEP meetings, and conferences, carve out some time to connect with your teammates on a social level. On a Wednesday or Friday night, set aside some time to have a 30- to 60-minute virtual gathering to talk about things unrelated to school. If the conversational road turns down Work Avenue, it's OK; just don't stay on that road for too long. Speaking from personal experience, we can say that some of the best work relationships are fostered during time spent outside of work.

SPEAKING FROM EXPERIENCE:
Observations from Michael and Nita

Michael's Observations

It was Tuesday, March 17, 2020—St. Patrick's Day. We were called into an emergency meeting for the third time that week. This time the situation seemed a little more serious. The coronavirus was taking center stage globally. What we thought was a discussion about the possibility of missing a few days or even a few weeks of school would soon turn into something straight out of a science fiction movie.

Our principal stood in front of us and explained how the district would be moving to a virtual format. School was fully "going virtual." An older, veteran teacher muttered, "How the hell are we supposed to teach, let alone reach our students now?" You could hear hushed discussion among the teachers and staff. Everyone felt it: a collective W-T-H! There were so many questions. Teachers were noticeably worried and some appeared scared—for themselves, their colleagues, and especially their students. I overheard one teacher say, "School is their only outlet. How will they be able to do this?" Some teachers talked about how they would be able to accomplish so much more by working from home, but some paraprofessionals were crying, asking if they would be out of a job because they would no longer be able to help in the physical classroom.

So many concerns and emotions filled the room. The laundry list of unanswered questions about the children, their families, teaching methods, expectations, and the potential duration of our new virtual reality was immense. There was a mad rush to create worksheet packets for parents to pick up. Regardless of the circumstances, we would prepare work for our students.

It was a surreal time. Most of us were a little shell-shocked, but some found time to fully embrace self-care during the pandemic—including in the form of lying on the beach during normal school hours. This approach to self-care made it hard for teachers who were doing what they were actually supposed to do during the school day. In moving forward, it made it almost impossible for educators to work from home, which meant they had to enter the school building to teach virtually. Needless to say, I remember it all: the good, the bad, and the funny. It was something none of us had ever experienced before.

Nita's Observations

For me, it was Friday, March 13, 2020. The district had sent an email telling us that we were going to be virtual for the next week of school. They told us to pack up the things that we needed in order to teach virtually. However, the kids had been sent to the bus without any of the devices they would need to be able to learn virtually. Teachers were panicking and stressed. Our administration let us know that we would have to have devices picked up by families the following week.

At first, to be honest, teachers were happy for the break. March is a long month, and getting a week "off" was just what the doctor ordered. What we didn't realize was all the confusion that would follow—issues with Wi-Fi, lack of Wi-Fi, and consistency in how teachers would approach a new way of teaching. What we didn't realize is that tons of worksheets and packets that may have initially not been acceptable learning tools for students would now be OK to send home for students to complete. What we didn't realize was that we were going to be out for the rest of the year.

Yes, I remember that day. I also remember the teachers who were extremely resilient. I remember those who continued to maintain strong relationships in spite of the circumstances. I remember the ones who reassured their students that things would be OK. I remember the ones who dropped off worksheets, books, and supplies to students' houses. I remember the teachers who remembered that relationships are the foundation that sustains us through even the most difficult times.

Reflective Questions

- Do you remember when you were told your school would be transitioning to a virtual teaching environment? How did you feel?
- Do you think your school district helped you prepare for that moment?
- What do you know now that you wish you had known then?
- How successful was your virtual teaching experience?
- What was your biggest takeaway from this unexpected virtual teaching experience?
- What are some areas where you could grow in your virtual teaching?

9 Closing Thoughts

We cannot overstate the importance of building relationships in schools—with *all* stakeholders. Regardless of your position or contribution in the school building, your relationships matter. After all, more than any other factor, relationships determine whether you stay or you leave.

As we wrote each chapter, we wanted to thoroughly explain and expound on each respective relationship. Although we knew that particular chapters would resonate with certain readers more than others, we wanted each chapter to describe a relationship that plays an equally pivotal role in the daily functioning of schools across the globe.

Relationships can be a polarizing topic within some educator circles. Some believe too much emphasis is placed on relationships. However, many successful educators, educational researchers, and recent data identify relationships as a primary contributing factor in thriving schools. Even though relational work can be challenging, we want educators to remember that relationships can ultimately carry you through those difficult moments, help you remember your "why," and bring a level of joy made possible only through established ties.

As lifelong learners and forever educators, we also wanted to highlight what we've learned along our journey in the education profession, reflecting on personal experiences near and far. We hope that our deeper conversations and individual perspectives strike a familiar tone with educators. We sincerely hope you enjoyed this book (our first) and want to leave you with one last observation from each of us.

SPEAKING FROM EXPERIENCE:
Observations from Michael and Nita

Michael's Observations

Never in a million years did I think I'd be writing a book, but once the pandemic hit, it became so clear. I wish I could say I had a grand epiphany or an inspirational story that just leapt out at me, but it really wasn't like that. It was actually more like a conversation with Nita that went like this: "Hmm, babe. I think we may be onto something. Think we can make a whole book out of it?" From that conversation, we were off and running—or, more accurately, off and writing!

Although neither of us is a "traditional" relationship expert, we both had our experience in the school building where, we could argue, we were experts. We worked in different capacities, which meant different perspectives. I don't recall any special technique or Jedi mind-control trick that seemed to always lead to success in our work. It came back to the relationships that had or had not been established.

Throughout my life, I've always found relationships to be one of the primary cornerstones in success, longevity, and safe work environments. Professionally, I've conducted countless mediations, de-escalations, and counseling sessions, and I've delivered professional development on the power and importance of relationships. Personally, I've always believed relationships make the world go 'round, turn enemies into allies, and have the power to transform any situation. The key is building, maintaining, and restoring.

Nita's Observations

When thinking of how this book came to be, I can't help but recall the many conversations that Mike and I had about various relationships in the schools in which we worked. We had many after-work conversations about relationships that sustained us, relationships that made us want to hang up our hats, and relationships that were nonexistent. We often discussed the importance of these relationships and ways to build, maintain, and restore them. Although we didn't use that particular terminology then, that's what we were discussing. We were thinking of ways to lay a foundation—a foundation that we knew had to be there in order to cultivate joy in this field.

As we've repeatedly stated in this book, one thing we know is that relationships take work. It's not always easy, and there were times in my own career experience when I wanted to throw in the towel. I wanted to give up because of my frustration or anger, or even sadness. But I also knew the passion and love I had for this work. I knew and still know the difference that I wanted to make in the lives of others. I wanted to make a difference in the lives of students, families, teammates, colleagues, and even the leaders that I worked under. That was my driving force, my passion, and I would even say my purpose.

Is this work in education sometimes hard and overwhelming? Absolutely. Are there aspects of the field of education that we want to change? Definitely. But one thing I have learned in my 18 years in this field is that without continued work on the foundational factor of relationships, we cannot bring about change. So yes, this work is life-changing for ourselves and for those we work with—each and every day.

Acknowledgments

The COVID-19 pandemic brought about a plethora of challenges and crises. Somehow in the midst of the chaos and uncertainty, we took time to reflect. We reflected on our experiences and how we could best influence education outside our small sphere of influence. *Every Connection Matters* is a work we were destined to create together. We want to take the time to truly thank Franchesca Warren, Alfred Brooks, and Wade and Hope King for giving us the initial platform in the edu-conference space. It provided a much needed space to recharge during times of mental, physical, and emotional exhaustion in the education profession.

We have been blessed to know and work with some exceptionally talented educators. We thank you for your enormous contributions—the "in the trenches" work that only educators know. On behalf of that student whose heart and family you touched... thank you.

We know that we stand on the shoulders of countless educators who have done and continue to do the work of pouring into students, teachers, and leaders each and every day. We have worked alongside and learned so much from these educators. Our hope is that this book is affirming to those already doing this work and that it spotlights areas in which the work needs to be done.

In addition, we have immense gratitude for members of the editorial team at ASCD, including Stephanie Bize, who helped to bring our work into fruition, and Liz Wegner, for their belief in us and in the necessity of this work, their ongoing affirming and constructive feedback, and the constant communication throughout the production of this book. We appreciate you for helping us to find the North Star in our journey.

Last but certainly not least, we are so grateful for our families who encouraged and supported us through our long days of writing, allowing us uninterrupted (or sometimes interrupted) time to plug away on our computers to manifest this work. We are forever grateful that they allowed us to ask questions about relationships in schools and their experiences and offered listening ears. You are our anchor in this work and the heart of what we do each and every day.

References

Ansari, A., Hofkens, T. L., & Pianta, R. C. (2020). Teacher-student relationships across the first seven years of education and adolescent outcomes. *Journal of Applied Developmental Psychology, 71.*

Baker, L. (2020). Self-care amongst first-year teachers. *Networks: An Online Journal for Teacher Research, 22*(2).

Barth, R. S. (2006). Improving relationships within the schoolhouse. *Educational Leadership, 63*(6), 8–13. https://www.ascd.org/el/articles/improving-relationships-within-the-schoolhouse

Burns, A. (2022, January 7). Building trust with students—even before class starts: How to promote psychological safety in your classroom. *Harvard Business Publishing.* https://hbsp.harvard.edu/inspiring-minds/building-trust-with-students-even-before-class-starts

Chapman, G., & White, P. (2019). *The 5 languages of appreciation in the workplace: Empowering organizations by encouraging people.* [Audiobook]. Oasis Audio.

Creekmore, M. E., & Creekmore, E. (2020, August 13). Back-to-school self-care: Putting your oxygen mask on first. *Pear Deck.* https://www.peardeck.com/pear-deck-blog/2020/8/13/back-to-school-self-care-putting-your-oxygen-mask-on-first

Damascan, I. (2019, September 4). What emotional connection really means in relationships. *Medium.* https://medium.com/relationship-stories/what-emotional-connection-really-means-in-relationships-acd1408fcc6e

Ed Trust & MDRC. (2021, May 27). The importance of strong relationships. *The Education Trust.* https://edtrust.org/resource/the-importance-of-strong-relationships/

Flook, L., Goldberg, S. B., Pinger, L., Bonus, K., & Davidson, R. J. (2013). Mindfulness for teachers: A pilot study to assess effects on stress, burnout and teaching efficacy. *Mind Brain Education, 7*(3).

Freudenberger, H. J. (1974). Staff burn-out. *Journal of Social Issues, 30*(1), 159–165.

Freudenberger, H. J., & North, G. (1985). *Women's burnout: How to spot it, how to reverse it, and how to prevent it.* Doubleday.

Gehlbach, H., Brinkworth, M. E., & Harris, A. D. (2012). Changes in teacher-student relationships. *British Journal of Educational Psychology, 82*(4), 690–704.

Gentile, D. A., Sweet, D. M., & He, L. (2019). Caring for others cares for the self: An experimental test of brief downward social comparison, loving-kindness, and interconnectedness contemplations. *Journal of Happiness Studies, 21,* 765–778.

Goleman, D. (2007). *Social intelligence: The new science of human relationships.* Bantam Books.

Good Therapy. (2022, January 31). What's the connection between physical health and mental health? https://www.goodtherapy.org/blog/whats-the-connection-between-physical-health-and-mental-health/

Greater Good in Education. (n.d.). Positive staff relationships: Why are they important? https://ggie.berkeley.edu/school-relationships/positive-staff-relationships/#tab__2

Hopkins, M., Bjorklund, P., Jr., & Spillane, J. P. (2019). The social side of teacher turnover: Closeness and trust among general and special education teachers in the United States. *International Journal of Educational Research, 98*(1), 292–302.

Knopf, H. T., & Swick, K. J. (2007). How parents feel about their child's teacher/school: Implications for early childhood professionals. *Early Childhood Education Journal, 34*(4), 291–296.

Law, B. F., Siu, A. M. H., & Shek, D. T. L. (2012). Recognition for positive behavior as a critical youth development construct: Conceptual bases and implications on youth service development. *The Scientific World Journal.*

Le Cornu, R. (2013). Building early career teacher resilience: The role of relationships. *Australian Journal of Teacher Education, 38*(4).

Marzano, R. (n.d.) Tips from Dr. Marzano: Delivering on the promise. *Marzano Resources.* https://www.marzanoresources.com/resources/tips/dotp_tips_archive

Mayo Clinic Staff. (2022, August 3). Exercise and stress: Get moving to manage stress. https://www.mayoclinic.org/healthy-lifestyle/stress-management/in-depth/exercise-and-stress/art-20044469

Mendler, A. N. (2001). *Connecting with students.* ASCD.

Men-Tsee-Khang. (2015, June). *Gangri langsto.* Tibetan Medical and Astro. Institute.

Olender, R. A., Elias, J., & Mastroleo, R. D. (2010). *The home-school connection: Forging positive relationships with parents.* Corwin.

Oxford Languages. (n.d.). Relationship.

Pierson, R. (2013). Every kid needs a champion. [TED Talk]. https://www.ted.com/talks/rita_pierson_every_kid_needs_a_champion

Rimm-Kaufman, S., & Sandilos, L. (2015, March). Improving students' relationships with teachers to provide essential supports for learning: Applications of psychological science to teaching and learning modules. American Psychological Association. https://www.apa.org/education-career/k12/relationships

Shaikh, H. (n.d.). Culturally responsive family engagement. *Parent Powered Creator of Ready4K.* https://ready4k.com/blog/education-equity/culturally-responsive-family-engagement

Sparks, S. D. (2019, March 12). Why teacher-student relationships matter. *Education Week.* https://www.edweek.org/teaching-learning/why-teacher-student-relationships-matter/2019/03

Streeter, L. G. (2021, October 18). Why so many teachers are thinking of quitting. *The Washington Post.* https://www.washingtonpost.com/magazine/2021/10/18/teachers-resign-pandemic/

Suni, E., & Vyas, N. (2023, June 23). Sleep hygiene: What it is, why it matters, and how to revamp your habits to get better nightly sleep. *Sleep Foundation*. https://www .sleepfoundation.org/sleep-hygiene

Valosek, L., Wendt, S., Link, J., Abrams, A., Hipps, J., Grant, J., Nidich, R., Loiselle, M., & Nidich, S. (2021). Meditation effective in reducing teacher burnout and improving resilience: A randomized controlled study. *Frontiers in Education, 6*.

Waddell, J. (2010). Fostering relationships to increase teacher retention in urban schools. *Journal of Curriculum and Instruction, 4*(1).

Wang, M. C., & Haertel, G. D. (2000). Teacher relationships. *Spotlight on Student Success*. Laboratory for Student Success. http://msan.wceruw.org/documents/ resources_for_educators/Relationships/Teacher%20Relationships.pdf

Will, M. (2021, September 14). Teachers are not OK, even though we need them to be. *Education Week*. https://www.edweek.org/teaching-learning/teachers-are-not-ok-even-though-we-need-them-to-be/2021/09

Index

The letter *f* following a page locator denotes a figure.

About the Authors

 **Michael Creekmore** is a licensed professional counselor with more than 15 years of experience and certified professional counselor supervisor, working as a professional school counselor, freelance writer, public speaker, and voiceover artist. He earned his bachelor's degree in experimental psychology from the University of South Carolina and his master's degree in counseling psychology from Clark Atlanta University. Michael has also served as clinical director and clinical supervisor to community mental health programs and has been an independent consultant for the past 15 years. Throughout that time, he has supervised, educated, and assisted in the development of younger clinicians. Michael has always promoted maximizing clinician opportunity through experience and leveraging expertise. In his free time, he enjoys spending time with his family and friends, attending his kids' extracurricular activities, writing, and purchasing sneakers. Michael is also a self-care advocate and enjoys traveling whenever he and Nita get an opportunity to do so.

Nita (E'Manita) Creekmore is an instructional coach, presenter, writer, and inclusive literacy advocate. She was in public education for 18 years, teaching elementary grades for 13 years before becoming an elementary school instructional coach for 5 years. Nita obtained her bachelor's degree in English and master's degree in elementary education from the University of South Carolina. She also received her educational specialist degree in educational leadership from the University of Virginia. Nita truly believes that in all aspects of the education field, relationships must always come first. She is passionate about being an advocate, support, and thought partner for teachers in order to give students what they need. In her free time, she loves spending time with her family and friends, attending her kids' extracurricular activities, practicing yoga, writing, and relaxing with a good book. Nita believes in maintaining a healthy work/life/personal flow.

Together, Michael and Nita own Creekmore Conversations, where they collaborate with schools to cultivate strategies to build, maintain, and restore relationships. They have four children, three daughters and a son, and live just outside Atlanta, Georgia.

Related ASCD Resources

At the time of publication, the following resources were available (ASCD stock numbers in parentheses).

All Learning Is Social and Emotional: Helping Students Develop Essential Skills for the Classroom and Beyond by Nancy Frey, Douglas Fisher, and Dominique Smith (#119033)

The Classroom Behavior Manual: How to Build Relationships with Students, Share Control, and Teach Positive Behaviors by Scott Ervin (#122033)

Committing to the Culture: How Leaders Can Create and Sustain Positive Schools by Steve Gruenert and Todd Whitaker (#119007)

C.R.A.F.T. Conversations for Teacher Growth: How to Build Bridges and Cultivate Expertise by Sally J. Zepeda, Lakesha Robinson Goff, and Stefanie W. Steele (#120001)

Facilitating Teacher Teams and Authentic PLCs: The Human Side of Leading People, Protocols, and Practices by Daniel R. Venables (#117004)

Forces of Influence: How Educators Can Leverage Relationships to Improve Practice by Fred Ende and Meghan Everette (#120009)

Keeping It Real and Relevant: Building Authentic Relationships in Your Diverse Classroom by Ignacio Lopez (#117049)

Powerful Student Care: Honoring Each Learner as Distinctive and Irreplaceable by Grant A. Chandler and Kathleen M. Budge (#123009)

The Principal as Chief Empathy Officer: Creating a Culture Where Everyone Grows by Thomas R. Hoerr (#122030)

Still Learning: Strengthening Professional and Organizational Capacity by Allison Rodman (#121034)

Taking Social-Emotional Learning Schoolwide: The Formative Five Success Skills for Students and Staff by Thomas R. Hoerr (#120014)

Teaching with Empathy: How to Transform Your Practice by Understanding Your Learners by Lisa Westman (#121027)

We Belong: 50 Strategies to Create Community and Revolutionize Classroom Management by Laurie Barron and Patti Kinney (#122022)

For up-to-date information about ASCD resources, go to **www.ascd.org.** You can search the complete archives of *Educational Leadership* at **www.ascd.org/ el.** To contact us, send an email to member@ascd.org or call 1-800-933-2723 or 703-578-9600.